To Susan
with love,
mom
(Feb. 1996)

4"

* * * * * * * * * * * *

YOU
SET MY
SPIRIT
FREE

* * * * * * * * * * * *

Rekindling the Inner Fire Devotional Series

REKINDLING
THE INNER FIRE

♦ ♦ ♦ ♦ ♦ ♦ ♦ ♦ ♦ ♦ ♦ ♦ ♦

YOU SET MY SPIRIT FREE

♦

A 40-Day Journey
in the Company of

JOHN OF THE CROSS

Devotional Readings Arranged
and Paraphrased by

David Hazard

♦

BETHANY HOUSE PUBLISHERS
MINNEAPOLIS, MINNESOTA 55438

Published by Bethany House Publishers
A Ministry of Bethany Fellowship, Inc.
11300 Hampshire Avenue South
Minneapolis, Minnesota 55438

Printed in the United States of America

Library of Congress Cataloging-in-Publication Data

John of the Cross, Saint, 1542–1591.
    [Selections. English. 1994]
    You set my spirit free ; a 40-day journey in the company of John of the Cross ; devotional readings / arranged and paraphrased by David Hazard.
        p.   cm. — (Rekindling the inner fire)
    1. Spiritual life—Catholic Church—Prayer-books and devotions—English. 2. Catholic Church—Prayer-books and devotions—English. 3. Devotional calendars. I. Hazard, David. II. Title. III. Series.
BX2179.J63213   1994
242—dc20   94–38330
ISBN 1–55661–481–0   CIP

To
Richard Foster
and
Linda Graybeal

Foreword

For all our talk of "freedom in Christ,"
Christians today are nearly as trapped by the
world and our own flesh as anyone else. Anxiety,
addictions, burnout, failure, disappointment—is
this what Jesus meant for us to inherit when He
offered us peace? when He attracted us to the life
of a Christian, saying, "You will know the truth
and the truth will make you free"?

Have we found the truth that sets us free? We
need more than right Christian doctrine. We need
to actually experience freedom *from within*.
Freedom from destructiveness toward others and
our own selves. Freedom from sin, which turns
us against God and men.

John of the Cross was a man, a powerful
spiritual light in sixteenth-century Spain, who
found that freedom. Like a pioneer who searches
for water amid the same wastelands where others
have failed, John discovered an unfailing stream
of the Holy Spirit exactly where it was
promised—"hidden with God in Christ."

You Set My Spirit Free, the seventh devotional
book in the REKINDLING THE INNER FIRE series,

introduces the spiritual path to freedom that was discovered by John of the Cross. Before reading the following brief sketch of John's life, you must know why a strong dose of John's writings is vital to reviving your spiritual health.

There is a lot of confusion among Christians today about spiritual-life writings like those of John of the Cross. Some would lump Christian meditation and silent contemplation with Eastern and "New Age" counterfeits of the same practices—which is like saying devout Republicans are the same as devout Chinese communists because both tend to wear pants every day. This view looks only at the external, not the internal and eternal realities.

John is a master of spiritual devotion—devotion, that is, to the true Way of Jesus Christ.

Throughout the ages, many Christians have found this same wellspring of inner life—proving that Jesus was no liar. His promise of "life flowing from within" is truly possible. We can immerse ourselves in the "river of life" because it continues to flow like a spring from its Source—that is, the Rock, the Life, the Way: *Jesus*. He remains steadfastly where He has been since His bodily ascension to the right hand of the Father—hidden in plain view.

Fortunately, men like John of the Cross, and others, left "maps" for us to follow, to help us on our way to the promised life of true freedom in the Spirit.

John of the Cross was a man whose life underwent a radical transformation when he experienced a rare taste of the Spirit of God.

He was born Juan de Yepes, in the Castile region of Spain, in 1542. A generation or so before, Torquemada's Inquisition had forced the family to convert to Judaism—quite possibly, it had also stripped the family of economic advantages. John's father was a poor weaver, who died while John was a little boy. His mother was left to work the looms, and as John grew he struggled from trade to trade, trying his hand at the hammer and saw, the paintbrush, and the tailor's needle.

When his mother moved the family from their small country village to a nearby and more prosperous town, young John was forced to become a professional beggar of sorts. Hired by a charitable hospital for syphilitics, John roamed the streets asking alms for the sick. Was it out along the twisting cobbled ways of old Medina del Campo that John first heard the inner "call" to devote his life to Christ? to forsake worldly possessions and career for the love of God?

We can imagine the sights and sounds of old Spain and how they gripped the adolescent boy: the music and poetry that boiled in Spanish blood, spilling into guitarsong in the streets. Nightly, the young suitors sang out their passions beneath the verandas of darkly beautiful and wealthy women, with all the exaggerated romantic lingo of those high medieval lovesongs: *I die for love of you! Your beauty surpasses all other beauties!*

What we do know is that John—ragged and penniless—was also gripped by a passion, an intense devotion. He was given some schooling by the local Jesuits. But it seems that, alone on those streets, bound by poverty and a fairly hopeless future, he felt a love . . . caught an inner vision . . . of Christ, the eternal Lover of our souls.

Some kind of alluring warmth radiated from this young man. We know that something extraordinary transported John for perhaps the first time, in spirit, above the mean, gritty world of begging and the streets. Nowhere did he record or report many of the supernatural events that attended his otherwise simple, devout, personal life. And later, when others witnessed miracles in John's presence—*this is important*—he urged them to overlook the miracle, to tell no one about it, and to fix their eyes on the spiritual love of God that is ours in Christ.

What we do know is that he was captured by some overpowering experience of the love of God, and it forced him into a lifelong mission—a quest to find words to *explain* the heights and depths of God's holy love . . . how the fire of this love comes to us . . . how we enter into its consuming flames. And in all of his writings he would stay true to that paradox of the spiritual

10

life: *God's love is offered freely; to experience it costs us everything.*

So here was a young man whose inward vision was simple of the path that leads into the fiery heart of God's love. His spirituality is not for super-saints or initiates of mystical knowledge. But at times he could only express it in love poetry, as in his *Spiritual Canticle*, so inspired by the *Song of Songs* and yet so powerfully original. It is the cry of the Bride, searching for the Lover, whose presence can be felt, and who is invisible:

> Where have you hidden away?
> You left me weeping for you, my Love.
> Wounding me, you then vanished
> like a stag; I ran to find you,
> calling after you—but you were gone. . . .

> Reveal your presence to me
> and kill me by your gaze and beauty.
> See how my suffering for your love
> is only cured when you—
> or your face—comes near to me.

Fortunately, in this young man God carefully mingled two streams of spirit—like fine wines blended in the same bottle. He was given a clear-thinking mind, and of all the devotional writers, none is more mystical *and* more supremely logical. For this reason, and others, we can trust him to guide us carefully between the wretched excesses of either one of those ruts.

His teachers recognized both John's fire of

devotion and his piercing intelligence. After some years of schooling, he was offered the chaplaincy of the hospital. Had he not gone on, however, to study at the university in Salamanca, which was one of Europe's finest institutions, we might never have received more than the devotional poetry—which would have been gift enough. But he mastered the fine points of logic, making his works like *Dark Night of the Soul*, *Ascent of Mount Carmel*, and *Living Flame of Love* supreme among Christian writings.*

At twenty-one, John joined a spiritual order known as the "Carmelites" because they practiced prayerful contemplation, solitude, a life free of possession—living together in the tradition of Christian men and women of earlier centuries who joined in communities in the wilderness of Palestine. I should say, this is the way the Carmelites were supposed to be living. By John's day, the order had fallen into a pathetic state of worldly decay. Solitude and prayer were replaced by gabbing. The parlors of Carmelite homes hosted gossip-fests. The commitment to frugal living was replaced by wheedling for fine gifts from wealthy patrons. Love trysts were common. In short, it was one of those sad periods in Church history—in some ways, like our own.

---

*For full treatments of these three works, I recommend E. Allison Speers excellent translations. *Dark Night* is available from Doubleday/Image, and the other two from Triumph Books.

One woman had begun, with quiet determination, to bring reform. No matter how you present the need for renewal, however, it comes as a slash against the *status quo*. Theresa of Avila was that kind of sword in the hand of God. "His Majesty"—which is how Theresa referred to the Lord—had also broken her heart by touching her with His presence. Her mission was nothing more or less than to beg Christians to turn back to the simple, freeing love for God.

For this edged message Theresa suffered an angry backlash from her "brothers and sisters in Christ," because her call to a devoted life cut into the consciences of monks, nuns, and quite a few bishops too.

When John met Theresa in 1567, it was like two forest fires converging. John left his order to join Theresa in her reform movement—taking the name *John of the Cross* as an emblem of his purpose and devotion. The cross is exactly what he would have.

It is miserable to contemplate the opposition and suffering John faced from the Church until the end of his days, all because in his Scripture-teaching missions he called Christians to practice unbroken fellowship with God. On the other hand, the light of God's love does require us to gradually let go of our fearful grip on the world, and to move out of our self-centeredness in all of its deceptive forms. Face the fact: Light always hurts, and then it heals. So before we condemn

John's contemporaries let us allow his thoughts, as they are arranged here, to search our hearts for these forty days. Then we'll see. . . .

John would be twice kidnapped by emissaries of the Church. Once, as fellow Christians were breaking down his door to arrest him, he fled to his room to hide or destroy writings—not to protect himself, but for the safety of others who might suffer just for having heard or read his words. Theresa desperately appealed to authorities during his imprisonments, saying she would rather he'd been captured by the Moors than these Christians. For good reason. In one captivity, John was viciously beaten with leather belts, almost daily, by whole roomfuls of men. His shoulders were left painfully crippled for good.

Like the apostle Paul, though, something extraordinary would happen to John through all this intense humiliation and suffering.

Once, he was locked for almost six months in something like a broom cupboard where he could not even stand upright. He was not allowed a change of clothes or water to wash, until his skin crawled with lice and his muscles were locked in cramps. He nearly froze in winter, and the stifling summer heat almost smothered him.

One oppressive midnight, a breath stirred against his face, coming perhaps not from anywhere in this world. In the darkness, he saw new light. From pain and wounding, love was kindled . . . words came. . . .

On a dark night, kindled in love with yearnings—
oh! happy chance—I went forth without being
observed, my house being now at rest. . . .

These words were the kernel of spiritual
teaching he would labor to share for the rest of
his days. It was John's mission to explain how a
Christian can live in spirit above the "dark night"
of our natural senses—to put to "rest" our
striving and complaints so we can "escape" from
the imprisonment of our fallen flesh and walk
freely with God, above pain, above sin and self.

Practically speaking, the voice actually
instructed John, as it were, on how to escape
from his cell. He would run scot-free into the
world's night . . . but more importantly, he would
be free within.

John spent the rest of his days, though,
teaching others how to walk in the love and
presence of God—occasionally protected by a
benevolent bishop here or there, but mostly
hounded by those who wanted to torture and
silence him.

John fled from town to town across southern
Spain on the back of a donkey. As he traveled the
open roads, the breathtaking Sierra Nevada range
accompanied him, lifting his soul with views of
white-capped peaks and cascading pure waters.
The inspiration surely found its way into the
Ascent, John's signature teaching.

Wherever John went, teaching on the love that

is ours in the presence of God, miracles began to happen. His message was simple and, as with all the great spiritual teachers, everything in it began with God and not with self-centered man:

> God is our "mountain"—immoveable and unfailing. He calls us to come and "ascend" in His Spirit above all earthly care, limitation, pain, and sin.
>
> God sends His Holy Spirit, issuing as from a hidden wellspring on high, to refresh and strengthen us in spiritual "graces" to help us on our way—the path of humility, which is "the Way" of Jesus himself.
>
> God warms and lights us on our journey with His "living flame of love," giving us the inner strength to leave behind all that weighs us down, in order to follow the upward call.

In rare periods of official tolerance, the reform movement and John's teaching would advance in small bursts. But after Theresa died in 1582, the movement—and John's life—were pitched into turbulence. Friends turned against John, and destroyed even his personal letters. Many were imprisoned and died.

Despised and imprisoned again, John suffered isolation and a painful illness. His writings were being collected and destroyed. He died just before Christmas in 1591. The light and passion of one of the Church's greatest reformers had gone out . . . almost.

All of John's writings survived, hidden away in secret cupboards. But most important, the passion of devotion to God that he inspired could not be quenched. As it happened with so many, the official Church would soon recognize the power of God that was with him and claim him as its own true son.

Important to us are the promises we have been given by our Lord—*the promise of freedom in Christ, and life flowing from within.*

My prayer for you, as you begin this forty-day devotional experience, is that God himself will speak to your innermost being. Through the Scriptures and the words of John, may He show you how to rise above all that imprisons your soul. May His real presence dawn inside you again. May you rest only in Him, so your spirit can know true freedom.

All spiritual blessings to you, in Christ.

David Hazard
September 1994

Contents

YOU
SET MY
SPIRIT
FREE

1

Light at the Door

*All night long . . . I looked for the one my heart
loves. . . . [The Lover of my soul] thrust his hand
through the latch-opening; my heart began
to pound. . . .*

Song of Songs 3:1; 5:4

*But you are a chosen people . . . belonging to God,
that you may declare the praises of him who called you
out of darkness into his wonderful light.*

1 Peter 2:9–10

When God first breathes life into the body, it
is as if the soul were a blank canvas on which
nothing has been painted. From the time we are
children, our souls know nothing except what we
perceive by looking out through the "windows"
of our senses. So we grow to adulthood believing
that what we see and know through our senses is
all that there *is* to know.

But, in fact, as long as our soul is housed

within the body, it is like a prisoner fumbling about inside the walls of a pitch-dark jail cell, so far as spiritual understanding is concerned.

And even after we come to believe, and even after we hear the Word of God, we act like the blind and deaf much of the time. That is because no one has taught us that there is another way to perceive God—in spirit.

Before I say more about this, it is important that you establish this one truth about your soul: *Apart from God your soul is empty, without even a flicker of the Holy Spirit in it. And even after you come to believe, you will remain largely subject to this dark condition until the eyes of your inner man are healed and opened.*

For this purpose, the Holy Spirit is sent to blaze the light of truth into your soul. This spiritual light heals, and it shows us the way of freedom. For as long as we see only with our bodily eyes, we will continue to live like a blind captive, fumbling around inside a prison cell in the dark of night—while all the time *the door that leads to our freedom stands open.*

This is what I now propose: I will show you how to escape from this "dark night" of your imprisoned soul, to show you the way of faith that leads up into the constant light and love of God. Isn't this the cry of your heart—that God will show you an open door to himself?

Trust Him to lead you out of darkness, fear, misunderstanding, and doubt. For it is the light of faith that shows you the way of perfect freedom in spirit. Then you will find the thing your heart longs for—perfect peace and freedom in the presence of the Lord, who is the Lover of your soul.

ASCENT OF MOUNT CARMEL: BOOK 1, CHAPTER 3

My Father, you call me out to freedom. And I long to live confident and at liberty in you—not bound by all the things that hold me.

Now I hear you coming for me . . . turning the key . . . and I hear your voice calling to my soul, saying "Rise, and begin to walk with me to a new place."

Today, I commit myself to a journey that will lead me deeper in to your love. . . .

2
Waking

*I slept but my heart was awake. Listen! [The Lover of
my soul] is knocking: "Open to me . . .
my flawless one."*

Song of Songs 5:2

*I*f you are seeking after God, you may be sure
of this: God is seeking you much more. He is the
Lover, and you are His beloved. He has promised
himself to you.

In every quiet longing, you call Him. With
even your inmost prayer, you ask Him to come
near to you. Your true heart's desire is what
attracts Him, like a fragrance rising on the air. But
in your thoughts, you wonder if He hears you at
all. You must see the truth about this matter.

Our spirits are hungry and dry and weak.
Though we are wide awake, our souls, apart from
God, lie drained of all power and nearly asleep.
Then something stirs. His wondrous presence is
passing. Can you not sense Him right now?

The longing in your soul is actually His doing. You

may feel only the smallest desire for Him. There may be no emotion about it at all. But the reason your desire rises at all is because He is passing very near to you. His holy beauty comes near you, like a spiritual scent, and it stirs your drowsing soul.

I tell you again—it is not of your doing at all, this moment when your soul awakens. He creates in you the desire to find Him and run after Him—to follow wherever He leads you, and to press peacefully against His heart wherever He is.

These moments are also ordered of God, and are sent by Him in His timing. I am telling you this so that you will understand His spiritual laws by which He governs and calls out your spirit to himself. He whispers delicately all the while to your inmost being. And until now you have tried to follow Him on your own, and failed. Now He will show you how to follow Him *in spirit.*

What He wants, when you hear His voice, is for you to turn to the inner path—that is, to go to Him with all your need and miserable failure. Go and receive from Him forgiveness, goodness, and release from sinful desires. Receive His love. Press, and keep pressing into His heart, until you have pressed the image of His invisible nature into the substance of your soul.

For God desires that, in every encounter, our spirits become more like His. Then our old nature will be left behind, as we take on His new nature.

This is how we move in greater *oneness* with Him in all our ways.

God calls to you first, and awakens your desire for Him. But you must never make the mistake of rushing out of God's presence to try to do good, or to find freedom from sin on your own. You will fail. Let the Guide of your poor blind soul lead you first to himself. There you will receive His empowering grace (see Hebrews 4:16).

Do you think it is impossible that you, with all your flaws, can be changed into His likeness?

God offers to take you with His loving hand and lead you where you cannot go by yourself . . . along a way that no human eye can see, and that is the way of the Holy Spirit.

LIVING FLAME OF LOVE: STANZA 3

My Father, you call me your "flawless one." Before you I stand completely forgiven.

I am overwhelmed at your greatness—to think that my desire for you was really only a response to your whisper of love and longing for me.

Open my eyes to more of your wonders . . . as I silently wait before you now.

3
I Follow

I will get up now and go about the city, through its streets and squares; I will search for the one my heart loves. So I looked for him but did not find him.

Song of Songs 3:2

Follow the way of love. . . . Let love be your greatest aim. . . . Eagerly pursue and seek to acquire [the love of God]—make it . . . your great quest.

1 Corinthians 14:1; NIV, TLB, TEV

The light of God's Spirit is not the light of cold truth, which leads to the law and to judgment. [It] is a living flame of love. For love *is* the spirit of our soul's true Spouse. . . .

This flame of love is sent down to us from the Father of Lights (James 1:17). Isn't it love that bathes our soul, kindling a sense of awe and wonder at the glory of God? In this way, He refreshes us within by revealing His loving and gracious nature.

29

What I have just described is, in fact, the way the Holy Spirit begins His work in the soul. It is love that causes us to rise up from spiritual sleep and open ourselves to God. Love is the call; and love is the transforming power.

As we have said, God begins His greatest work when the inner man is opened to Him. He touches us with His Spirit, and His touch sends out "flames" that we perceive in flickers of holy awe, wonder, overwhelming beauty. God works to draw our will into His own, so that we come to want with all our heart to be made one with that flame—and the flame is *Love*. This is how the very life of God enters into us—when our old selfishness is consumed in the unquenchable love of the Father.

And the more we allow love to enter, the more we grow to love others with our whole will— even when they treat us miserably. In fact, God's aim is to change us from within so that it is the easiest thing for us to act in love at these times, whether we are overwhelmed with feeling for a person or not. Speaking and responding in love is most precious, because that's when we are fully open to God, obeying an action that originated in His heart. This is how His Spirit continually flows into this world—*through us*—to overcome the world's meanness.

I tell you, acting in love when others are not acting in love toward you—this is of the highest value to your soul. It is worth more than all the other works of faith you may have done, no matter how great they appear. Love is the highest aim, the greatest practice you can cultivate in your soul. It is the path on which you walk as closely as is possible to those who are already living in the life eternal.

The more we follow this path of love, the more our old self is consumed and dies—and the more God himself will be kindled in us. *God in us. . . .* His love will leap like flames of light and warmth through our words and actions, consuming our old vindictive ways of treating people. . . .

Some only have a taste for power and superiority. Some believe they must defend themselves at all costs. Their highest aim is to protect their flesh—that is, their pride, position, and security in possessions. These people do not have a healthy taste for the ways of God. To them, the way of love is bitter and foolish. Do not be like them.

Meditate on what I have told you, until the Holy Spirit opens the eyes of your soul, and you are convinced that what I am showing you is the path from death to life—the way of life that makes you spiritually alive in God.

LIVING FLAME OF LOVE: STANZA 1

My Father, Creator of Love and Light, how subtly I position myself at the center of all things.

31

And there, with defensive words or punishing silences, I barricade and protect myself against others . . . and mostly against you.

As I open to you, I ask you to wake all the darkened ways of my heart and consume any evil in me with your cleansing fire. Do not stop until you have reached the darkest, innermost place, so that I can see the truth . . . and learn how to live free from my self.

4
Living Love

Have you [completely] forgotten that divine word of appeal and encouragement?. . . . Submit to the correction and discipline of the Lord. . . . For the Lord corrects . . . every one whom He loves. . . . God is dealing with you as with sons.

Hebrews 12:5–7, AMP

I want to show you a marvel, a spiritual truth that will help you to understand the ways of God which the worldly-minded cannot understand:

The love of God is never idle, though our weak flesh often believes that He has forgotten us. We think the proof of His abandonment is that He allows unlovely things to happen to us. This is not so. But we misunderstand the way His love works.

God's purpose is to so enkindle us in love that we are full of life, and full of delight. But first, in order to penetrate into our souls, it is necessary for love to wound.

For God's love is both deeper and higher than

the poor sick thing we call love—which is not love at all, but walls of defense we raise about our inner man. And so we try to protect that which is in the throes of death, when Love wants to "wound" us and open us up to Life.

The sense of wounding we feel is really only the way our flesh *perceives* the first actions of God as He comes to join himself with us. And, in fact, these sparks of love may even feel to us like the piercing wounds of many arrows.

If you will seek Him in your spirit, I know that you will begin to see the pains and oppositions of life in this new way: They are the most tender and delicate touches of God's desire for us, by which He works the arts and wiles of love upon our soul.

You ask, "How can this be true?"

God must reveal to us that *nothing in this life is truly good, for it is not lasting.* And our soul, which is eternal, must stop trying to find its resting place and security in earthly loves and worldly joys. Nothing in this life can offer the secure hope, the limitless love our soul needs—for the earth and all that is in it is passing away, but our soul is eternal. . . .

Therefore, I say, renew your mind so that you come to see every wound that comes to you as coming from the playful hand of God. It is because He loves you that He refuses to let you rest your soul in this corrupt, dying world.

So I say—and now you will not think it is

strange—that God will wound you deeply. For in this way, He continues to open all the inner chambers of your soul. And the devil cannot enter there. And your own worldly senses, which would betray your heavenly Lover, cannot enter there.

In all this He is opening the way to the central chamber of your soul. There He plans to set before you a feast. This, I tell you, is the banquet place of the Holy Spirit.

LIVING FLAME OF LOVE: STANZA 1

My Father, I have sometimes blamed you when circumstances are hard, when I have felt wounded by other people . . . until I have felt bruised and empty.

Correct my spirit with your truth—that you are always at your work, in every situation, even those that hurt. And your greatest work is to free me from things that will always fail me in the end . . . so I can know your higher love that is endless. . . .

5
Through Thorns

I am . . . a lily of the valleys. Like a lily among thorns is my darling. . . .

Song of Songs 2:1–2

Then [Jesus] called the crowd to him along with his disciples and said: "If anyone would come after me, he must deny himself and take up his cross and follow me. For whoever wants to save his life will lose it. . . ."

Mark 8:34–35

*H*ow I wish we could understand, with our spirits, how to practice what our Savior counsels about learning to deny ourselves.

Let me warn you that there are many people telling us what it means to "deny ourselves"—but not all of them have spiritual wisdom and understanding of the road Jesus intended us to walk. His way is entirely different from what so many teach and, consequently, too many

Christians are led down the wrong path.

Some teach that we should withdraw ourselves from "worldly" people. Others say we must work hard to get rid of fleshly habits and sins as the right path to spiritual freedom. Still others are content to practice godly habits, pursuing a life of prayer and "putting to death" wants and wishes for material goods. Then there are those who follow the path of self-denial with sternness and severity, which has a certain look of zeal but is void of life.

None of these paths will lead to the total detachment from the traps and powers that are the real strongholds of this world. They will not make us free from having to fight to protect anything we think we own—even a right opinion. They will not lead to purity in spirit— that is, the freedom that comes as the old nature is consumed and dies and an entirely new life is formed in us. This is the path our Lord is pointing us to—which is the freedom to become *self-giving*.

If we follow the other ways I have described, we will mistakenly think we are growing strong spiritually, when, in fact, we are only feeding and clothing our old self-centered man with spiritual feelings. And that is like consoling a dying person with an imitation medicine.

Instead, we must follow God in the Spirit of Christ. And that means to strip ourselves of all things for the sake of walking in true communion

with the Father. For if we think He is merely
asking us to deny ourselves the comforts of
wealth and possessions, it will not even lead us
to the first step on the spiritual path. The way of
Jesus will lead us far beyond and above these
false beginnings.

The way of our Savior will lead to the
annihilation of all our *spiritual attachments*. The
fire of God must come to consume and cleanse
and purify inwardly.

No doubt you are wondering what I mean by
"spiritual attachments," and what it means to be
purified within.

By spiritual attachments, I mean the demand
for *only* the sweetness we sense at times in the
presence of God. If that is all we want, then we
will never grow strong enough to walk the true
and perfect path, on which God will lead us
through times of complete dryness of spirit, and
through distasteful trials that seem to overwhelm.

Dryness and despair and death will loom
again and again, and they will block us like
thorns from communion with God.

Again and again, your spirit will want to turn
and flee from these, its most terrible and
frightening enemies. But the spirit that would
grow stronger will let go and deny its own
demand for sweetness and comfort. I will go so
far as to say that we must turn from "spiritual
gluttony". . . .

Do we understand that there are only two

paths we must choose between? One is to follow
Christ through all thorns and learn all that it
means to deny ourselves and seek God, which
will lead us through the death of our old nature
and into the light of resurrection life. The other
path is to seek the fulfillment of ourselves in
God—that is, to seek only the blessings and
refreshment of God, *but not seek God for himself.*
This type of spirituality is the enemy of the cross
of Christ.

But, if our true desire is to have God
enthroned in us—well, that is all the difference.
When we want God above all, we are willing—as
Christ was willing—to follow in spirit, even in
the most dry and dark and painful of times. *This
is the love of God. . . .*

When you see with the eyes of faith that this
is the spiritual meaning of the cross, you will
know how to imitate Christ and do what He did.
You will take up your cross the way you take up a
favorite walking staff that you love to lean upon.
The cross will become your soul's true strength—
by which you learn to walk in God's presence.

ASCENT OF MOUNT CARMEL: BOOK 2, CHAPTER 7

My Father, Giver of all spiritual
blessings—stop me, Lord, when the outward look at
others causes me . . . to compare . . . and I measure
my well-being and progress by what I see in other
people.

Where I feel dryness of soul, show me if I hold on to a secret need to appear right and good and strong in the eyes of others.

Today, help me to imitate Jesus in spiritual dependence on you . . . seeking only to grow stronger in your purposes, no matter where you lead me.

6
Path of Faith

My Lover . . . stands beyond our wall
. . . peering through the lattice. . . .
"Arise . . . come with me."

———

Song of Songs 2:9–10

[Jesus said,] "The eye is the lamp of the body.
If your eyes are good, your whole body will be full of
light.
But if your eyes are bad,
your whole body will be full of darkness.
If then the light within you is darkness,
how great is that darkness!
No one can serve two masters. . . .
But seek first his kingdom. . . ."

———

Matthew 6:22–24, 33

When we begin the Christian life, we are so
blind to the things of the Spirit. As I have said,
the only "light" or understanding that enters the
soul, at first, is through our fleshly means of

"illumination"—that is, our sense of hearing, seeing, smelling, tasting, and touching. These are of no importance when it comes to spiritual perception.

Spiritual *sight* is what we need to walk in the Spirit, the way our Lord calls us to walk.

Let me quickly add that it is no good simply to "close our eyes" to the world around us, denying and rejecting "the world and the flesh." For a man who merely closes his eyes remains in darkness and is no better than a blind man who actually lacks in the ability to see. No, we must also have the eyes of our inner man—the eyes of faith—opened.

This is why David could say, "I am poor and needy. . . ." (Psalm 40:17), when it is clear that he was very rich, so far as worldly goods are concerned. The eyes of his inner man were not *set* on earthly wealth, so it was as though he really were poor—poor in spirit, as the Lord would have us. (And on the other hand, a man who is poor but has his heart and soul set on gaining wealth is not poor at all, but rich and fat in lusts.)

As you can see, the point is not whether we have wealth and material goods or lack them. We are not talking about *things* at all. For many are attached, as if by chains, to things they can never really own. I want you to know how to live in such a way that you are free from soulish attachments to anything this world has to offer.

I urge you to practice *spiritual detachment*—that is, to ask the Lord to carefully reveal to you every taste and desire you have for things of this world. As He does so, He will also help you to see that there is no true joy, and no lasting contentment or security in anything or anyone in this life. When this light, this eternal fact, begins to dawn you will find that your soul grows strong enough to walk the path of faith, free from all the invisible bonds that hold you as one kept in a dark prison. Our aim is always to become so free in spirit that it no longer matters whether or not we have the earthly things we crave.

Remember, it is rarely the things themselves that cause harm to your soul, for physical objects cannot enter into the soul's substance and cause actual damage. It is true, though, that the soul may be mesmerized by the world's offerings for a long time, and to wander far from the way of Christ.

In our fallen state, we will always be tempted to affix our soul to the world. Do not let your "eye" be drawn by the false "beacon lamps"—of wealth, or position, or fame, or possessions. Be vigilant over your will and desires, for these are the corrupt forces that dwell within, and keep you from living free.

And so, all that I will write to you will, in one way or another, be about this one thing: learning how to quiet your soul's natural hungers and demands for the things of this life—to pass through the dark night of the fallen soul—and travel on into the one true, burning Light.

I will describe to you how to continue in the soul's journey into loving oneness with God.

ASCENT OF MOUNT CARMEL: BOOK 1, CHAPTER 3

My Father—and Master . . . Heal my eyes. Sharpen my spiritual sight today, so I can quickly recognize what alluring things I pursue, before I am drawn away from the perfect path . . . which is you.

7
Real Presence

*By faith [Moses] . . . endured, as seeing him
who is invisible.*

Hebrews 11:27, KJV

Lie quietly . . . in silent meditation.

Psalm 4:4, TLB

*T*here is a clear line of distinction between
true faith, which is set on things above and
cannot be shaken, and the meager thing we *call*
faith, which rests on our human understanding—
and so it is a thing that is rooted in our life here
below. If you want to grow in spirit, you must
cross this line.

What we normally mean by faith is really
only our soul's ability to form thoughts about
God. As we said before, these thoughts are
based on the perceptions of our five fleshly
senses, coupled with our mental calculations
about God. This lower type of "faith" has

nothing to do with the ability to see with the eyes of the soul—which God himself must open up to us. The so-called faith that springs from our lower nature is related to human logic, which can never comprehend the true God, who is Spirit.

See how the worldly mind immediately recoils at such talk. No doubt, you want to object: "So, you're one of those 'otherworldly' and 'supernatural' people. Are you suggesting that I walk around in a spiritual haze? Faith has to be based on understanding, solid evidence, and logical truths—otherwise you're talking about something vague and purely 'mystical'."

Can we really comprehend God with our fallen human minds? No. Then how can we form true and accurate conceptions of Him? He is not a man—though in His drive and zeal to plant the heavenly seed of His living Word in our souls He is something *like* a bridegroom, and we are *like* His bride.

It's true, we do well to think on the effects we witness where His presence has passed. In this way we begin to comprehend some aspects of His nature. But if we use our reason alone to shape our understanding of Him, we will wrongly conclude that we "know" God. Then we begin to predict and limit what He will and will not do. This is dangerous ground, for in the end we are apt to dismiss Him altogether.

I understand how you might struggle with these thoughts. To the human mind, locked in its dark prison of perception, it is hard to step across the line from faith based on reasoned understanding into real, spiritual faith. Spiritual faith has silenced and blinded its own comprehension, and opened its inward eyes and ears to God as He is—transcendent, above all that we can think or imagine (see Ephesians 3:20).

The farther we withdraw, then, from our own understanding, the more our soul is freed to draw nearer to God himself, as He is, and not merely as we imagine Him to be. We draw nearer to God once we determine that our imaginations of Him are vain, and utter darkness—and the more we pass beyond these mental images by stilling our thoughts, the more we open our soul to His real presence.

Your natural mind will be troubled by this, because it is a spiritual means of progressing that challenges your soul's natural desire to seize control of everything, even your perception of God. If you follow this inner path of silence and stillness, you will understand what this means. And the Lord will quickly reward you with progress in deeper knowledge of himself.

LIVING FLAME OF LOVE: STANZA 3

My Father, ever-present . . . in a new way—in your way—begin to show me who you are. . . .

I quiet my soul before you now, asking you to let me know your Presence. . . .

8
Touch of Fire

I am my beloved's, and his desire is toward me.

Song of Songs 7:10, KJV

Because He is your Lord, bow down to Him.

Psalm 45:11b, NAS

Oh, the depth of the riches of the wisdom and knowledge of God! . . . I urge you, brothers, in view of God's mercy, to offer your bodies as living sacrifices, holy and pleasing to God—this is your spiritual act of worship.

Romans 11:33; 12:1

Determine in your heart that you want to reach the highest place in God. By that, I mean, learning how to live each day in pure, loving oneness with Him. And once you have set your heart on this upward path, you will have to choose it every day, and many times during each

49

day. For indeed your desire to rise to higher places in spirit will face many obstacles.

Now I will tell you about the first of these challenges, so that you will understand the operations of God's Spirit and not be discouraged when it occurs.

When you give your soul fully to God, and ask Him to transform you and flood you with His holy light, you are asking Him to fill your soul to its full capacity with himself—that is, with the living flame of His love. . . . Only in this way is it possible for the soul to find its way into a state of oneness with Him.

When His love first comes to us, we perceive it as a fire, and that is because His first work is to purify and cleanse the soul of sin and selfishness and fear and anger. Though this purifying and cleansing causes many to turn back, its purpose is to make us clear in spirit—clear as pure crystal, so that He may be seen in us.

At first, we resist His advance. But the more we allow Him to kindle His burning light within, the more it will drive out and replace the darkness there, until the light blazes out from within us, and with greater and greater intensity.

This is the spiritual height on which we set our hearts. Are you willing, then, to climb up out of your earthly darkness and move toward this high point of faith? For this is how the fire and light of God's love is centered in us, brilliant and bursting out from within.

I tell you, this is the manner in which the soul itself comes to stand more fully in God's fiery light—until we are consumed by Love. This is how it comes about that we appear to be wholly one with Him.

LIVING FLAME OF LOVE: STANZA 1

My Father, clean and holy—I know that I can never find my own way to the high peak of your love, but I know you can show me the way there . . . the way that Jesus walked.

Today, when my soul rises up against that one who tempts me to be impatient, demanding, superior . . . take hold of me. Embrace me in my weakness, and let me also give out warmth and light from your love.

9
Touch of Glory

*M*y lover is radiant. . . .
[His] love . . . burns like blazing fire,
like a mighty flame.

——

Song of Songs 5:10; 8:6

*W*e are . . . heirs of God
and co-heirs with Christ . . .
that we may also share in his glory . . .
that will be revealed in us.

——

Romans 8:17–18

*T*he highest purpose of a man or woman's soul is to be transformed into the spiritual likeness of Christ. . . . And by transformation, I do not mean a mere momentary change in appearance, but a change in the soul's *substance*.

This takes more than merely thinking or meditating on God, though it's true that even this ordinary joining of the soul to Him brings great benefit.

I have been talking about something greater—
that is, opening our innermost selves to the fire of
God's presence: *We must allow Him access to the
deepest places inside, where our true will and desires
dwell. It is there that He wants to kindle us with the
fervency of His love.* This is how—with our whole
being, mind, and might—we can begin to issue
out to those around us the living flames of love.
So, the soul has its first taste of the sweetness of
glory.

To this end, God sends the sweet flames of
His all-consuming love to refashion your
innermost being. This is the fire of God which
Isaiah saw in the Spirit, proceeding out of
Zion—that is to the spiritual dwelling place of
God. The flames are the Spirit's holy fire, which
flares with the power of a raging furnace from
the secret place of His temple in Jerusalem (see
Isaiah 31:9).

You may expect that as you open yourself
before God, the soul will be moved upon by these
profound, subtle, and sublime flames. This is the
glory of God, kindling within you. I tell you
truthfully, it is not actually possible to describe
the delight and sweetness of this divine
touch. . . .

But more importantly, as we are absorbed in
Him, submitting to the movements of His Spirit
He pours into us in loving wisdom, we are being
opened up to *Him.* We are purified and made
ready for His glorious entrance. For wisdom—

and the One who is Wisdom itself—"pervades and penetrates all things" (Wisdom 7:24).

LIVING FLAME OF LOVE: STANZA 1

My Father—"Opened to you . . ." and "touched by your glory." *I know this means more than having warm and pleasant feelings. . . . It means giving selflessly. . . .*

Teach me how to share the unselfish brightness of Christ. Remake me from the inside today, so that I look more like your Son, who is my Lord and brother. . . .

10
A Brilliant Darkness

Consuming fire came from [the Lord's] mouth. . . .
He parted the heavens and came down. . . . He made
darkness his covering. . . . Out of the brightness of
his presence [dark] clouds advanced.

———

Psalm 18:8–9, 11–12

*T*he soul that begins to pursue this higher way of God does not understand what is happening when the flame of God comes to purge him. So at first, in our fallen fleshly state, His cleansing touch does not feel sweet, but painful. If we understand His actions aright, though, and if we are willing to be patient under His hand, we soon find that His cleansing work in us is truly an act of friendship, performed by the hand of our soul's one true Friend.

In order for the flame of God's love to penetrate into the soul's substance, so that we may become *one with Love* . . . the Spirit's fire sets

55

upon the purpose of wounding the soul. Only in this way—painful as it feels at first—can He destroy and consume the imperfections and evil habits that sink their terrible choking roots into us. *Wounding, opening, cleansing, preparing us for the presence of God—this is also the true work of the Holy Spirit.*

I will say it plainly: The fire of Love that will afterward unite with the soul and bring it glory is the same fire which begins by assailing it in order to cleanse and purify. In order to picture this, think of the way that fire penetrates a log. As the flame begins it burns away the outer imperfections, stripping the log of scars and roughness. As its heat mounts, the fire penetrates into the log itself, until wood and flame are one. Just so, fire transforms wood into fire.

At first, as I said, the soul feels that God is subjecting it to so many terrible and trying circumstances. It suffers greatly, wondering if it is merely abandoned by God to great afflictions. From the depth of its being, the soul may overflow with emotion and weeping—for now the flame of God feels only oppressive.

During this time, as the Spirit prepares the soul for His coming in fullness, the fire of God is not bright but dark. . . . True, there are times when the heat of His loving advance feels sweet, but there are also times of inner torment and affliction. This is not at all pleasant, but rather makes the soul believe it is wandering in an abandoned and arid wasteland. The light shed upon the soul does not feel like the brightness of glory, but like a parching sun that is exposing the inner self.

The times of cleansing are full of bitterness and misery. As Jeremiah says, it was like "fire in my bones" (Lamentations 1:13). The soul feels confused, in the dark, not knowing what God is about—or if He is still there at all. . . . It wants to complain miserably like Job, saying, "Lord, why have you changed? Why have you become cruel to me?" (Job 30:21).

My description of this falls short of the reality, I can assure you. . . .

I want to strengthen you for such times with this knowledge: The dark fire of God is His remedy and medicine, which He gives to the soul to treat its many diseases. He does so, only to bring the soul back to health . . . to drive from it every kind of spiritual evil. It is no wonder that, at times, the heart feels as though it has been laid upon white-hot coals. . . .

LIVING FLAME OF LOVE: STANZA 1

My Faithful Father, I know that once you are in my life you will stop at nothing to free me from darkness . . . and even from those things that seem so good to me, but are not the best.

Thank you that you don't leave me when I resist

you and complain when you are doing your "dark" and deep-cleansing . . . and burning . . . work in me.

Today, I will stop my struggling and rest beneath all the healing operations of your hand.

11
Created Anew

Put off your old self,
which is being corrupted by its evil desires;
to be made new in the attitude of your minds;
and to put on the new self, created to be
like God in true righteousness and holiness.

Ephesians 4:22–23

Arm yourselves also
with the same attitude [as Christ]
. . . [do] not live the rest of [your] earthly life
for . . . human desires,
but rather for the will of God.

1 Peter 4:1–2

*M*any Christians find themselves in a place
they describe as "spiritual dryness." The
symptoms are these: restlessness, and a spirit
that cannot be consoled by the inner comforts
that once brought them peace.

And because these souls do not recognize

their true inner need, they mistakenly focus upon the outer trappings of the Christian life. They complain that "something is wrong" with other Christians, or with the faith itself. They are hungry and thirsty for something, but they do not know what it is.

This attitude is a type of spiritual greed. For many wrongly believe that they should always be experiencing newer and better delights of the soul. They may think that others are at fault for not attending to their spiritual needs, and for not giving them new and sweet truths, or new and exciting spiritual experiences. Though they do not see it this way, of course, they want to be catered to, fed just the right "spiritual delicacies" that will lift and delight their soul.

I warn you, guard against this wrong attitude about the spiritual life—that is, thinking that you must ever be seeking better counselors, new teachings, greater spiritual precepts, and reading book after book. These things may be good in and of themselves, or they may be in error. But even the best spiritual teaching will not benefit you at all if you are not growing and walking in the Spirit of Christ.

This walk in the Spirit begins when we begin to walk the path of Christ—the way of death and resurrection. By that I mean, we must daily seek the Holy Spirit's light and strength, so that we are "putting to death" the old way of living that binds us to our sinful, selfish inner man (see

Romans 6–8). Do you see that the honor and praise of men is *nothing* in comparison with eternity and the new kind of life—*eternal life*—that is offered to us now?

Empty your soul, I say, and seek to be filled with the attitude of Christ, which is a sure wellspring—unending, and brimming with life eternal. Count nothing as your own. Count all that the proud flesh desires as worth less than nothing. This is what it means to be "poor in spirit" (see Matthew 5).

If you miss this—which is our Savior's own spiritual way, and His first teaching—then you have bypassed the sure path to God. . . . I tell you, even the kind of spirit that wants to be sought and admired for its "great knowledge and spiritual insight" must be condemned. . . .

For true devotion to God comes when, with our heart, we keep in view our lowly, empty state apart from Christ. Walk in the light of this truth. Do not fix your affection on having any praise and glory here below. Make it your goal to become so emptied of self that you can be flooded by the presence and power of Christ that comes only from above (see Colossians 3:1–2).

Do you want to cross over to this kind of spiritual walk—which is the way He comes to dwell perfectly in us? Then your soul's demand that it be fed with spiritual delights must be killed. . . .

The only thing your soul may "covet" is to

have the same mind and attitude as Christ—to
live and walk with a right spirit before God. Then
you will know that you are pleasing to Him.

DARK NIGHT OF THE SOUL: BOOK 1, CHAPTER 3

*Father of Life, I do want this new kind
of life in the Spirit that you offer. But you ask me to
leave my dry and empty self . . . when, Lord, self is all
I have!*

*Help me to leave behind my own dry springs of
fearful and self-serving interest. Lead me to the river of
your Spirit, the current of clear goodness that flows
without ceasing. . . . Help me just once to step into
your unfailing new life, so that I will want nothing
else.*

12
Rule of Life

*J*esus replied, *"The kingdom of God does not come
with your careful observation . . . the kingdom of God
is within you."*

———

Luke 17:20–21

*L*et the peace of Christ rule in your hearts.

———

Colossians 3:15

God is alive and present in the very
substance of the soul—even the soul of the
world's greatest sinner. This primal kind of union
exists between God and every creature. For it is
God alone who preserves their very being, and if
He breaks this bond their life ceases at once (see
Psalm 104; Colossians 1:15–17).

When I speak of union with the Lord, though,
I am speaking of an entirely different kind of
oneness. Because God's living Spirit is a river of
life, issuing in graces, He will always forge these
essential bonds with His creation. The oneness

63

we may enjoy with the Lord comes as the soul is transformed into His likeness through union with Love. . . .

This kind of union is above all natural desire. It is supernatural. It comes to pass as two wills— that of the soul, and that of God—are joined into one, and there is nothing in either one that is repugnant to the other.

This is why the soul must allow itself to be purified completely of selfishness and sins that are displeasing to the Lord—that is, of anything that keeps the soul from being conformed to His image in love. For it is the pure love of God that transforms. . . .

Therefore, the soul must first be stripped of all that is in it by nature—stripped of its own small and self-centered ways of looking at the world, stripped of the strengths by which it tries to shape everything and everyone to its own will. Only in this way can all that is *not* of God be cast out—all the secret stubbornness that refuses to conform to His image!

See this clearly: Our soul is constantly in a struggle to control and conform the world to our own image and will. This power within us—this *secret will* to take over God's place of rulership— must be cast out. Then we can receive His spiritual likeness, and be changed.

So while it is true that God is in every soul, giving it breath and preserving its very being by His living presence, yet He is not freed into every soul to have His dominion over it, and those souls never awaken to the life that would cause them to rise above their fleshly nature.

Clearly, there is a spiritual kingdom that we may enter. And this kingdom announces itself in our souls as we open up to God's limitless love and grace. So we must strip ourselves of the desire to stay bound up in others—that is, in our striving to have others love and esteem us as we believe we *must* be loved by them.

The more we choose to live by our old habits, the more we are held tightly by these unhappy bonds, and the more we hold others in this trap with us.

In this way, we grow farther from oneness with God.

ASCENT OF MOUNT CARMEL: BOOK 2, CHAPTER 5

My Father, when I think I am growing stronger in you . . . I catch my foot against an obstacle in my path, and stumble. Looking down, I see it is a hardened bit of my own will.

I know that in any kingdom there can be only one ruler. Today, help me to choose wisely who will be the ruler of my life . . . governing in graces.

I will let go today, and allow you to rule.

13
Power of Grace

No one can lay any foundation other than the one already laid, which is Jesus Christ . . . [the quality of our spiritual workmanship] will be revealed with fire. . . . My conscience is clear, but [my good conscience] does not make me innocent. It is the Lord who judges me . . . [the Lord] will bring to light what is hidden in darkness and will expose the motives of [our] hearts.

1 Corinthians 3:11, 13; 4:4–5

As many as received him, to them gave he power to become the sons of God. . . .

John 1:12, KJV

God's intent is to reveal himself to the inner man by grace, the way a freshwater spring opens up and flows from a crack in the dry ground.

This is what the apostle John meant when he told us that we would receive "power to become the sons of God." If we receive Him within—in

His Spirit of holiness, beauty, love—then we are transformed in God. This can only happen for those who are "born of the will of God" and not merely "of blood" (John 1:13). For there is nothing in our natural fleshly makeup, nothing in even the best human personality, that can accomplish this change in Godlikeness.

No, our transformation into the image of Christ cannot be accomplished by the workmanship of our natural man—not even if we try with the whole power of our human will. For the will is subject to a fleshly manner of judging what is good or bad, right or wrong. And the will is also subject to our limited way of comprehending and understanding—that is, through the senses only—and it can never grasp all the many strands and higher purposes God weaves together in any one act, setting in motion new plans here, bringing an end there to other plans He set in motion long ago.

And so the power to become sons of God does not come from trying with our human will to act in a godly manner. Our new birth comes as we are changed by the inward actions of *grace*.

Grace gives us the courage, strength, and boldness to let our old way of seeing things and our past way of dealing with life be put to death. Grace opens the eyes of the soul to the high holiness and beauty and transcendent wisdom of God—the way of life that is above (see Proverbs 15:24). Then, in spirit, we learn how to live and to "walk" above every natural event—those that torment and confuse, as well as those that woo and lull us to sleep in the comforts of this world's life.

Grace is the touch and movement of God's living power within. This allows us to know that we have been reborn, and that we are adopted as His children. The life of grace far surpasses mere mental belief in the truths of God—it frees the spirit to fly powerfully above all things, with a kind of inner life that is beyond description.

As John says elsewhere, "No one can see the kingdom of God unless he is born again" (John 3:3). To have our spiritual sight restored is to understand the spiritual way of life. That is, we must bring our fallen soul into the quiet rest of "death," trusting and at peace in the hands of God. Then the Holy Spirit can raise us to a new type of life that is directed and proceeds from within. And so the soul begins to become like God in purity. . . .

In order to help you better understand this new birth, I will make a comparison.

Imagine a ray of sunlight as it touches a pane of glass. If the window is clouded with mist, or with streaks and stains, the rays of light will not be able to illuminate the glass perfectly with its wonderful brilliance. This is not because of the quality of the light. But if the pane of glass is cleansed and free of impurities, then a transformation takes place. The light catches the glass, and it is as if the fire of sunlight is burning within the heart of the glass itself.

In reality, glass and light remain separate and distinct in nature. Yet the glass takes part in the light, and in this way appears as one with it.

The soul is like the pane of glass. And it is the light of God's Life—the Spirit and Being of God—that must rise like a new morning within that soul. In this way, God comes to dwell.

ASCENT OF MOUNT CARMEL: BOOK 2, CHAPTER 5

My Father, *I see in me a desire to "own" power and ability . . . to be strong and capable in and of myself, which keeps me from growing in dependence upon you.*

I come now, to stop and rest in your beautiful and revealing light. . . .

Is it power I seek? Or your grace to become?

14
God's Work

Jesus said to them, "My Father is always at his work to this very day, and I, too, am working."

John 5:17

For Wisdom, the fashioner of all things, taught me. In her is a spirit that is intelligent, holy, unique, manifold, subtle, ever-moving, clear . . . loving the good. . . .

Wisdom 7:22, New Oxford

As we have seen, the soul must be awakened—reborn—from its natural perceptions and way of living. . . .

When we are awakened in the Spirit, we see that God never sleeps (Psalm 121:2–5), and that He is always moving about His work to shape and arrange events in His wise government of our lives. . . .

Now, as we awaken in spirit, God begins to draw back some of the "veils" of misperception that have, until now, blinded our spiritual eyes to Him. He shows us His true nature. And though not all the veils are drawn away and we "see through a glass, darkly" (1 Corinthians 13:12, KJV), we *are* able to see this most important truth: *He looks upon us in compassion, His eyes brimming over with flowing grace.*

Do we understand the fullness of grace with which He looks over every event that concerns us now? . . .

No, I am afraid that at first our understanding is still somewhat darkened. For we think that our turning to God, our crying out to Him, has nudged Him awake toward us, as if He had been sleeping. In fact, it is quite the opposite: It is our soul that has been awakened by the movement of God.

It is important for you to understand this truth—that our lives are moved under the all-wise directing of God. For if we are not careful, our old manner of thinking will allow us to continue believing that we must somehow make God wake up—by our prayers and "good" behavior—and get Him to move on our behalf.

Isn't that the way our lowly, self-centered nature works? We believe that others have the same motives we have, and that they think and act just as we would. So we judge others—and even God—by the way we think and behave. Our views are so limited! We judge by ourselves, and

71

not from a higher perspective outside ourselves. . . .

Therefore, because we are so prone to neglecting and forgetting about the needs of other people, we think that God is capable of being slothful toward us. And so we accuse Him of neglecting us when circumstances become painful, or simply not to our liking. Even David spoke out of this low-minded blindness when he cried to the Lord, saying, "Awake, O Lord! Why do you sleep? Rouse yourself!" (Psalm 44:23). In this moment of frustrated blindness, David attributed to God the weak characteristics of a fallen man. . . .

May God himself awaken your sleeping soul, so that you see with the eyes of faith the multitude of excellent virtues that are found in Him. May He wake you—those who have ears to hear—with thousands and thousands of voices, each one shouting about one of the countless ways that He and all His works are good . . . and *only good*.

LIVING FLAME OF LOVE: STANZA 4

*M*y Good Father, thank you that you are never asleep . . . that you are alert and at work over all that concerns me.

One by one by one, help me to see all the goodness that is coming to me from you . . . the goodness that has already come . . . and the goodness I have yet to see because I am blinded by my own frustrations.

15
Stillness

You are weak in your natural selves. . . .

Romans 6:19

Be still before the Lord. . . .

Psalm 37:7

"That which is born of the flesh is flesh. . . ."
So our Savior told us. And "that which is born of the
Spirit is spirit."

John 3:6, KJV

There is a fine cut revealed in the Scriptures—a division made by the very Word of God himself, the One who wields perfectly the living sword of the Spirit. Pay close attention.

Our first joy, excitement, and love for God generally springs from our fleshly nature. We may feel, with senses tingling, the lift and the wonder of His presence. Because these feelings

74

are aroused in the presence of God we can mistake them as a quickening of the Spirit. In fact, they are sensual and come from the lower nature. What is born of this nature is doomed to die. Only what is born of the Spirit can lead us into greater growth in the nature of Christ. . . .

This kind of growth comes only as we learn to pass out of the "dark night of the soul"—that is, to be still and walk free from all the fleshly feelings, perceptions, will, and our faulty ways of imagining what God is like. For we must silence the lowly human senses of the flesh that lead us to false conclusions about God, and keep us blind to His constant work and movement all around us. We come to a place of inner stillness, much like the silent calm of night that settles just before dawn . . . then we perceive the first true-dawning light of God's Spirit.

With patience, care, and practice, the soul can learn to disregard—to "put to sleep"—all sensual feelings of love. These will always fail you, because they are rooted in your failing lower nature. This kind of "love," which is sensual and not spiritual at all, must be brought under control. . . .

Unfortunately, there are many believers who never learn how to move beyond this state—it is a kind of "spiritual lust," because it enslaves them to the senses that demand to be gratified. When their sense of delight with spiritual things dries up, they are full of grumbling, discontent, and even bitterness toward God for "abandoning" them.

Ask yourself whether you have experienced this sort of thing: Perhaps you have just spent a pleasant time at prayer and worship. You felt that your soul was focused in the light of God . . . at peace and feeling delight. You leave and go about your business, and it is not long before the lightness is gone. You feel irritated and disappointed with God, the way a small child fusses when it is taken away from the breast and sweetness of its mother.

Do not feel condemned. There is no sin in recognizing your soul's infant state. But is this how you want to continue—in immaturity? Or do you wish to escape from this demanding babyhood, to grow strong and constant in the Lord?

At first, as I have told you before, the flame of purging will feel painful to the soul. And your fleshly nature will wring and struggle and complain and demand that God "prove" His presence with consoling sweetness. Would you forever give in to a child's whining and demands for sweet treats? Do not give in to your soul's demands of "sweet blessings" from God either. For that will only make it weak and sick.

Your soul will live and become stronger as you choose to make it walk steadily, even when your soul is like a wasteland. Turn your soul, I say, to walk toward God when all seems blackest and there is no light of His presence to be seen anywhere. Though this seems harsh at first, you will soon understand how this journey through dryness and darkness is God's chosen way of purging your soul of its need for lower, sensual joys . . . false joys that always fail.

Dark Night of the Soul: Book 1, Chapter 6

My Father, I have always thought that growing stronger in spirit would mean becoming invincible . . . beyond need. Now I see that you are teaching me to receive another kind of strength when I come to the end of mine.

Teach me to walk in your ways as I have never known them before.

16
Approval

Confess your sins to each other
and pray for each other. . . .

James 5:16

I want to call your attention to those times
when someone misunderstands you, or
disapproves of you. Their disapproval makes
you very uncomfortable. In fact, what you feel
is the fire of God, touching you inwardly,
revealing how anxious you are to be approved
by man.

Let's say that the disapproval comes from a
spiritual leader. You begin to fret, and say, "He
has misunderstood me." Then you begin an evil
attack. You watch his behavior and notice all that
is human and fallible, and you decide, "He is
really not *spiritual* at all. Why did I think God
could use him to counsel or guide me in the first
place?"

You can hardly stand it. Eventually, you
move on in search of someone else who can

counsel and guide you in a way that feels more comfortable—that is, you want to be encouraged according to your own tastes. Do not become this kind of person, whose spirituality is thin indeed.

I want you to see that the natural man in each of us does not like to be challenged. In fact, we do not at all like others to think less of us. And is it not true that we absolutely hate to see the deeper truths about ourselves? We only enjoy talking with those who will praise us for how well we are already doing. And—no small coincidence—this also builds us up in our own eyes.

Yes, we run, as we flee from death itself, from anyone who causes us to see our weaknesses and errors. But this is exactly what we need to shake us out of our self-centeredness and self-satisfaction. Only then do we stand a chance of being driven back onto the safe road, which is the way of Christ.

Examine your heart. Do you carry secret ill-will toward those who misunderstand you?

Perhaps they are the very ones whom God has sent to expose your pride. Or have you become full of presumptuous sins—that is, presuming that you know what is best for you? Unchallenged, and left to ourselves, we become puffed up. We become full of words, commitments, and resolutions—which we can walk away from and forget. Then we grow fat on our own spiritual opinions, which we freely share.

Disapproval, misunderstanding, rejection—these are the very circumstances that have the power to make us more like Christ. But if it comes to that, we are really not so willing at all!

Do not allow secret pride to make you its captive. Do not make it your real goal to be approved by others for being such a wonderful spiritual man or woman. . . . Choose the safe road.

Regarding spiritual mentors, I say, seek the honest views of men and women who will not be impressed by your outward shows of "goodness." Mere flattery and comfort will blind you. Your one desire should be to remain on the low and lighted and good path of humility.

Be on guard, then, against your soul's desire to depend on the good opinions of others. And also your soul's tendency to influence others only to think highly of you. In fact, stop tallying up the compliments and words spoken in support of your "goodness." Keep no such accounting at all. . . .

DARK NIGHT OF THE SOUL: BOOK 1, CHAPTER 2

My Father, I want this kind of freedom . . . not an arrogant freedom in which I think I am

above the opinions of other people . . . but the real
liberty that comes from knowing my heart is open—no
matter what is said about me—to listen only for your
voice and your opinion.

17
Inner Sight

[Jesus said,] "Wisdom is proved right by her actions."

Matthew 11:19

Humility . . . comes from wisdom. . . .
But the wisdom that comes from heaven is first of all
pure. . . .

James 3:13, 17

If by the Spirit you put to death the misdeeds of the
body, you will live, because those who are led by the
Spirit of God are the sons of God.

Romans 8:13–14

The light of God goes beyond understanding scriptural doctrines. His light is meant to dawn within you, so that you embrace with your heart the truth of God, and find it coming alive inside you. Then you will know how to shut out the voices of the world—keeping your eyes of faith focused on God, and keeping your inner ear tuned only to His voice. In this way, you will know that He is infusing you with spiritual sustenance that refreshes your innermost soul.

If you learn how to walk this way of the Spirit, you will be free of those soulish means of trying to "work up" a spiritual feeling. For we must learn that the "works were finished from the foundation of the world." And "we which have believed do enter into rest" (see Hebrews 4:1–6, KJV). In fact, it is by entering this inward rest that we gain the strength to rule over all circumstances, whether good or bad. . . .

It is a great accomplishment for a soul to learn this walk in the Spirit. No wonder, then, that as the soul is learning to move on this spiritual path it meets such terrible opposition. This resistance often comes in the form of the most trying temptations, and these can go on for a long time.

Some of the most devout seekers-of-God, for instance, can be attacked by vile and unclean thoughts—a lustful spirit—even during the very act of prayer and devotion. Before the eyes of their imagination comes a parade of immoral images, things they had never dreamed of in their lives. This abominable spirit torments them more than the pangs of death.

For others, the attack comes as a blaspheming spirit. It whispers to the soul inconceivable lies about God—or shouts them into the soul at unexpected moments, to render the soul weak through the terrible inner stress of fighting off such horrendous slanders.

Another abominable spirit that can come to molest us is what Isaiah called "a perverse spirit" (19:14, KJV). This spirit tortures the most sincere seekers of God by crushing them with scruples— that is, by causing them to pick over and become anxious about every "secret motive," until they can bear their own thoughts no more. Or else it tangles them in religious perplexities. And soon their ability to judge is wracked and confused. This is one of the worst horrors, for it feels as if you have lost your way and become no better than any hell-bound and benighted soul. . . .

No doubt you will recoil at my next words, but I tell you the truth so that you will not turn back when such temptations come: The Lord himself allows these inward trials. It is His way of causing us to see that our own fallen understanding of the spiritual way is bound up in our attempts to purify and perfect and to be strong in ourselves. But when we are overwhelmed by these attacks, we may finally cast ourselves in total dependence upon His benevolent wisdom and deep understanding. For He alone knows what will cause us to discover how to walk in the Spirit.

This type of wisdom must be born in us from above: Our fleshly strengths must be proven to be weakness; our present understanding must be proven to be blindness. Then we can walk in wisdom, that is, in the realm of those who know and see and have their strength in the Spirit.

Be comforted in knowing this: These greater trials of the soul are measured out by the loving hand of God. And He only permits them to come upon us to the degree of self-dependence and self-righteousness that must be purged from our soul.

DARK NIGHT OF THE SOUL: BOOK 1, CHAPTER 14

My Pure Father, I have so often been distracted in prayer, and given up. I ask you to surround me as I bring my soul to the quiet place where I can meet with you.

Today, before I struggle for answers . . . before I act . . . let me be still. I want to receive your wisdom and insight that come, pure-fallen, from above.

18
Pruning

[Jesus said,] "I am the true vine, and my Father is the
gardener. He cuts off every branch in me that bears no
fruit, while every branch that does bear fruit he prunes
so that it will be even more fruitful. . . . No branch
can bear fruit by itself; it must remain in the vine.
Neither can you bear fruit unless you
remain in me."

———

John 15:1–2, 4

And this is my prayer: that your love may abound
more and more in knowledge and depth of insight, so
that you may be able to discern what is best and may
be pure and blameless until the day of Christ, filled
with the fruit of righteousness. . . .

———

Philippians 1:9–11

Walking in the Spirit will teach our soul how
to overcome three of the deadliest sins. The sins I
am referring to are *anger, envy, and unwillingness to
obey the Lord.* These run like veins of imperfection

through the substance of our stony sin-hardened soul, to its eventual crumbling and ruin.

It is the cleansing, purging work of God to take out these "flaws." He takes the soul through many hardships, and through times when it feels dry and lifeless.

"To what end?" you ask. In order to show us that our anger, envy, and disobedience to Him come from one and the same source—by that, I mean our soul's desire to find its ultimate happiness, consolation, and security in this world. This, of course, can never be.

So God must show us the great darkness we are in when our soul tries to find spiritual nourishment here, where there is no life. And it is our blind soul's demand and frustration that causes these sins to grow and bring forth their ugly fruits in us.

How marvelous is His ability to raise from within us a crop of righteousness—virtues that are exactly the opposite of the thorns and tares which once grew rampant in the miserable depleted soil of our soul. He uses His "tool" of trying circumstances to crack our hard ground. He plants His Word of light in our deep darkness. He pours the living water of His Spirit on our dryness . . . and the soul softens.

This is how He roots out anger and generates a harvest of humility in us—so that we come to rest in God's providence and power and not our own, which also makes us gentle, kind, and respectful toward our neighbors. It is how He destroys envy—that unhappy disturbance that rules in us when we decide that what we are and what we have is not as good as what God has chosen to give others. And by His actions, He raises a harvest of joyful obedience in place of our complaining nature—that is, our desire to quit the spiritual life when, day by day, we must behave as children of God, set apart for His use, when everyone else seems to get by with such ungodly behavior.

As God's Spirit cultivates this new type of life in us, the only envy we will experience is a longing to be more like those who exhibit humble obedience to Christ. And He uproots our old sluggishness and complaining about obeying God, when that means passing up comforts and pleasures. For He has revealed the endless crop of boredom we will harvest when we base our life on pleasure-seeking—instead of sowing acts of goodness and love for a harvest of eternal life.

I urge you: Quiet the complaints of your soul, and put down its rebellions, for it will naturally want to turn back to its old pleasures and demands. God will, He *must*, bring this utter dryness upon your soul in order to kill these deadly roots of sin.

When all within you is dry, when your soul is begging and tempting you to turn back to the world and all its creature comforts—in *that* moment, quiet its pathetic demands. In the time of empty, silent, desert dryness, *fix your soul on God alone.*

You can hardly imagine the harvest of lasting joy that will come to you when you learn to be free from your soul's whining and wheedling. For then, God himself can speak quiet words, and you will know as never before the sweet tenderness of His great love for you.

Each time this dryness comes—and it will come back with greater ferocity, like a consuming hot wind—stand your ground and endure in quietness of soul. The reality of God's presence will come to you, and each time He does your inner man will perceive more of His transcendent beauty than your natural mind can imagine.

DARK NIGHT OF THE SOUL: BOOK 1, CHAPTER 8

My Father, you who are the Good Gardener . . . When my circumstances seem hard . . . when people let me down . . . I will look above these things to you.

Give me the courage to accept the "pruning" you want to do in my life now . . . so I will soon produce a greater crop of righteousness for you.

19
Servants

Do not deceive yourselves.
If any one of you thinks he is wise
by the standards of this age,
he should become a "fool"
so that he may become wise.
For the wisdom of this world
is foolishness
in God's sight.

———

1 Corinthians 3:18–19

Jesus answered, "You would have no power . . .
if it were not given to you from above."

———

John 19:11

Wickedness cannot begin to grasp goodness.
And on our own we cannot comprehend how to
grow and live in oneness with God. For He is
supreme goodness.

Nothing in the world's wisdom, nothing in
our human knowledge or abilities, can match the

wisdom of God which is eternal and from above. In comparison, our so-called wisdom is utter ignorance. . . .

In the eyes of God, people who think themselves as owning great wisdom and insight are like foolish children—ignorant, really, except for the knowledge that someone else has taught them. So they have no reason for acting puffed up, as if they are so wise and knowing. . . .

Do not let yourself be drawn into this kind of foolishness and pride. Live every day in the knowledge that every bit of spiritual insight is a pure gift from God. The only way to receive wisdom from God is to come before Him in spirit as humble, simple, ignorant little children—for that is what we are.

Push away every bit of understanding you think you have gained and, each day, offer yourself as a servant who is willing to do the lowest job He bids you without question, and without feeling you should be "promoted" to a higher position, where you do not need to serve others any longer because you "know more than they do" about spiritual matters. . . .

In order to live and walk in the light of God's higher ways, set out each day as if you know absolutely nothing—for we must never assume we know what God wants to do and exactly how He means to do it. If we assume, we become as servants who have taken over their master's house, until they wind up complaining and incensed with him because they think they know how to handle his business best, and they speak impatiently about him as if he is just a silly buffoon.

That is miserable service, indeed, in which our soul chafes under the most agonizing and powerless type of slavery: "If only we could make the Master see it and do it our way!" Getting free from such a spirit of "superior knowledge" and "lordship" is what we need.

It is part of learning to walk in the incomparable freedom that comes when we let go of any higher position we have usurped, and live simply, under the loving direction of the Spirit of God.

As long as you allow this insidious desire to secretly overtake you—that is, the desire to be master of your own soul—you will be as powerless in spirit as a slave, always subject to your lower nature. . . . In this state, how can your soul ever experience the liberty that comes from the Spirit?

ASCENT OF MOUNT CARMEL: BOOK 1, CHAPTER 4

My Wise Father, over and over I find myself believing I know what's best for me, and cannot understand why you won't move into action on my behalf when I pray.

Have my prayers just become demands—in which I ask you to help me accomplish things as I see fit? Let me sit at your feet again, with a new willingness to hear and obey—to do the things you see fit.

20
True Righteousness

[J]esus said,] "Unless your righteousness surpasses that of the Pharisees and the teachers of the law, you will certainly not enter the kingdom of heaven."

Matthew 5:20

Seek righteousness, seek humility. . . .

Zephaniah 2:3

Some people want God to remove their sins and imperfections from them for the wrong reason. And you may well wonder how wanting to have your sins taken away could spring from anything but a good motive. I will tell you.

Quite simply, if God helped some people to overcome sin, they would become more proud and presumptuous than they already are in their secret heart of hearts. For though many Christians do not realize it, their motive for wanting to become free from imperfections *is* wrong. They want to achieve the sense of righteousness that comes—a false sense, really—when you think you have gotten the better of sin. Then you wrongly think that you no longer have the need to cast yourself on the mercy of God each day, where, knowing your real weakness, you can draw upon His grace and power over sin. . . .

From this hidden pride—truly invisible to so many well-meaning Christians—numerous other serious sins grow. And these souls are greatly harmed, even as they think they are becoming so good. . . .

But those who want to go on proceed in a different manner and with a different kind of spirit. They know that they must live every day in an attitude of complete abandonment to God—that is, in an attitude of humility. . . .

These souls recognize what God has done for them in His tremendous love, and they know how great is the darkness that is in them. They know how much God deserves of them—their whole-hearted allegiance—and that anything they could ever do for Him is very small in comparison with His willingness to die for them. So they are not trying to work for God in any way to "satisfy" Him, or to buy His good opinion of them. They serve out of love, and in their hearts they know it is little enough. . . .

In this way, they learn to train their eyes on the Lord, on His mercy and His goodness, and not on themselves. And they are also kept—great

freedom indeed!—from turning a judging eye
toward the successes and failures of others.

DARK NIGHT OF THE SOUL: BOOK 1, CHAPTER 2

*My Father, thank you that you want to
set me free from a position I am not equipped to hold—
that of judge. Thank you for opening my eyes to the
truth that when I step into the role of judge at all,
secret pride comes in . . . and love goes out.*

*Today, I will hold a "fast" on criticalness. . . .
Help me to act and speak only out of compassion, and
to leave the judging and the outcome to you.*

21

Serving . . .
With Joy

*Y*ou have stolen my heart. . . .
How delightful is your love. . . .
Let my lover come into his garden. . . .

Song of Songs 4:9–10, 16

*M*ary . . . sat at Jesus' feet, and heard his word.
But Martha was cumbered about much serving. . . .
Jesus said unto her, Martha, Martha, thou art careful
and troubled about many things: But one thing is
needful: and Mary hath chosen that good part, which
shall not be taken away from her.

Luke 10:40–42, KJV

*Y*ou may be the kind who resists the idea of
"advancing" in spiritual growth by means of
contemplation—that is, by quieting your soul and
by emptying yourself of lower concepts of God,

so He can reveal himself to your spirit as He really is.

Perhaps, when you hear someone speak of contemplation, you think, "It's impossible to love and obey someone if you don't understand clearly who they are and what they are like. Isn't it better simply to school your will to obey God—whether you understand Him or not? Is it not true that too many people merely enjoy pleasant feelings about God, but it never changes anything in their will—so in the end they really do not obey Him?"

You are right, in one sense, to think this way. For when it comes to the tasks we must perform in this world we must serve God with all our might.

And yet, there is another way to comprehend God—to know Him and His ways—that surpasses years of struggling and trying to understand who He is and what He asks of you in service to Him.

Allow Him to infuse into your soul *His* breath of eternal life, *His* light of knowing, *His* fire of love. This is nothing like striving with your mind to understand Him, not at all like generating kind Christian acts out of a good and willing determination to obey Him. It is letting Him come in to the inner chambers of your soul and to show himself to you.

Oh—the sudden burst of brilliance that comes when our soul's Creator speaks His Word within!

In any explosion, light bursts out together with fiery heat. In the same way, the true light and knowledge of God himself releases in the same instant the heat of love. So love *and* understanding of God are infused into the soul at once.

It is impossible to fully explain exactly what takes place in this, the soul's encounter with its Lover. Can an earthly lover describe in words what occurs in his heart when his beloved is near? Could he if he tried? And would he even want to tell you?

In the soul's most delicate communions, there is light and love beyond telling. You know that this is true.

LIVING FLAME OF LOVE: STANZA 3

My Father, whether you allow me the special sense of knowing you are with me today, or whether I do not sense your presence at all, I will trust you to lead me in the simple acts of kindness, service, and compassion . . . which mark your footsteps.

22
Shepherds

The Lord . . . makes me lie down in green pastures,
he leads me beside quiet waters,
he restores my soul.

Psalm 23:1–3

I will begin to tell you of three blind guides who can mislead you. . . .

There are many spiritual shepherds of God's flock who do not understand those who are moving in to the prayer of quiet and of oneness with God. It is important for you to know this, for one of these well-intentioned people can greatly hinder your spiritual growth.

Some of these shepherds understand the ordinary type of meditation—that is, mulling over doctrinal truths, or even letting their imaginations re-create some scene from a story in Scripture. But in truth, not many take the time to cultivate their souls with even this simple practice, though Scripture itself directs us to do so. Sadly, many spiritual leaders have become merely preoccupied

and distracted with "the business of their flock."
(And, of course, most other Christians are
likewise caught up with the affairs of this life,
too.)

Therefore, I find there are many spiritual
shepherds who judge the spiritual growth of
others by themselves—even though they
themselves feel overwrought, overly critical, dry,
and often verging on hopelessness. They have
not escaped the trap of sensuality—that is, the
bondage to feelings and the lower perceptions we
have been describing. They have not learned the
way of escape from this lower path, which is so
full of snares (see 1 Corinthians 10:13). And so
they cannot imagine that there *is* a way—or that
an ordinary person could find it when they, the
spiritual ones, have not found it.

As the apostle Paul says, these people do not
understand the things of God (see 1 Corinthians
2:14). Nor do they see the towering pride that
stands within themselves: Imagine!—a simple
Christian thinks he knows something of God's
ways beyond what they know! So they have
already made up their minds, and they refuse to
listen with the ears of the soul when a simple
person speaks to them about learning to find rest
and peace in the ever-flowing love of God.

Secretly, these people are thinking, *Pure
idleness!* And what they will tell you is, "Yes, it
would be nice if we had the luxury just to bask in
God's goodness. But He requires hard work—

service and obedience." As if either practice—
growing deeper in a state of restful inner prayer,
or faithful service—was ever intended to replace
the other.

How tragic that these people who are
supposed to understand what it means to be a
shepherd of souls so often misdirect good
Christians, especially those who are inwardly
seeking after God! If a soul comes to them,
hungry and thirsty, all they know how to do is to
misdirect them—that is, to fill up their time and
their lives with more and more *activity*. They
drive true seekers to fill up their minds and their
souls with "spiritual words." They push them to
reason through doctrine. And they give them
many acts of service to perform.

And then these leaders wonder why their
followers come to them continually with the same
complaints—that the "spiritual life" has become
repugnant, that they feel dry inside, that they
feel driven and restless and scattered, as flocks in
a wilderness. This is tragedy indeed. For many
spiritual shepherds *want* to lead their sheep to
inner sweetness, but they do not know how to
find it themselves.

And the way to enter in to the quiet-flowing
waters of God, I tell you, is to progress each day
in opening yourself to the Lord. He alone can call
back together all the straying thoughts and
motives of your soul, and bring you to the place
of peace. . . .

Do not bypass this pathway, or you will be like those Christians who have sincerely professed their belief, but spend the rest of their lives feeling as unsure and striving as if they were still on their way to hell. . . .

LIVING FLAME OF LOVE: STANZA 3

My Father, you know I wander from you . . . sometimes forgiving, sometimes holding grudges . . . having confidence in you one day, and doubt the next.

I am so thankful that you know how to re-collect my straying thoughts and focus them on one path . . . trusting you to keep me in all my ways.

23
The Evil One

[T he man in the vision told Ezekiel,] "Where the river flows everything will live."

Ezekiel 47:9

[T he devil] ranks first among the works of God . . . under the lotus plant he lies, hidden among the river reeds in the marsh . . . [they] conceal him in their shadow. . . . When the river rages he is not alarmed.

Job 40:19–23, [John's interpretation]

Now I must warn you soundly of the second great threat to your soul.

On the road that leads from "walking in the flesh" to "walking in the spirit," the evil one brings his strongest opposition. For he works to keep you earthbound and weak. And you may well imagine that he wants no soul to find its way on this path of life, where you no longer rely on your own understanding (see Proverbs 3:5). Therefore, he wants to turn you back from this way of true ascendancy and strength in God alone.

His first lure is to make you expect to have "spiritual feelings." He is also a master at making even the most sincere Christians think that God will pour out on them all manner of material blessings. In this way, he gets many to rest and trust in their feelings of comfort. So comfort becomes the god of their souls, and not the true God who is higher than all.

How many souls are snared in this trap, baited with ease and good feelings! They think they have escaped the devil and have found the flowing waters of eternal life. But instead, they are caught right in his snare. With all the "evidence" of flowing blessings, they have no idea what they have lost—in fact, they believe God has come to move right in, bringing gifts! If they remain trapped here, they will never understand what it means to enter into their soul's innermost chamber with their true Spouse. Rather, they will remain standing at the outermost door of the soul—that is, the senses—and look out on the world thinking they are spiritual.

The devil is haughty, and Job warns us that he watches every pathway that would lead us to the higher life in the Spirit. Those who begin to regain their spiritual sight he attacks quickly in order to regain his rulership over them.

Let's say that, by chance, you receive a

moment of spiritual light from the Lord, showing you the inward path that leads away from the trackless wilderness of this alluring world. Well, the devil cannot stand to see your soul regather its lost sense of spiritual direction. He works doubly hard to ruin the Lord's work in you. How? By flooding your soul with horror, causing you to think of the losses and pains the Lord will "force" you to suffer if you give yourself entirely into His care.

Another of his stratagems is to watch closely as you enter into worship and prayer. Is it not at the moment of devotion that you find yourself strangely bombarded with all manner of distracting thoughts and confusions—and even real noises and interruptions?

Both are effective ways to draw you out from the interior sanctuary of the spirit. And when you have lost your concentration, he leaves you to wonder why you are such a failure, or why the Lord has abandoned you. With relative ease, he corrupts the way of many precious souls. . . .

And so we can understand what God says about the devil and his proud ways: The Lord says the devil shall drink up a river and arrogantly believes he can even swallow up the Jordan (see Job 40:23). For the Jordan is a symbol of the river of the Spirit that flows from the throne of God, in the heart of which we are borne up in the Holy Spirit's power (see Ezekiel 47).

No wonder he opposes us so. For to loosen

our sure hold on all that we know, and to be borne along in the currents of God's Spirit—this is how we come to have the very life of God flowing perfectly into us . . . and out through us to the world.

LIVING FLAME OF LOVE: STANZA 3

My Father, when I am dry and dead in spirit, show me if I have been obeying the whispers of the evil one . . . seeking your blessings instead of you . . . or pouring out criticism instead of encouragement . . . complaints instead of gentle words . . . gossip instead of prayer. . . .

Show me what spirit it is I allow to flow through me.

24
Like a Child

*[Jesus said,] "I tell you as seriously as I know how
that anyone who refuses to come to God as a little
child will never be allowed into His kingdom." Then
he took the children into his arms and placed his hands
on their heads and he blessed them.*

Mark 10:15–16, TLB

---

*I have stilled and quieted my soul; like a weaned child
with its mother, like a weaned child
is my soul within me.*

Psalm 131:2

The third blind guide that is a danger to your
soul . . . is *you.*

We think we are so knowledgeable about
ourselves and our own needs. More often than
not, we are just like a sightless and headstrong
person. We refuse help from anyone who could
tell us about deeper things of the Spirit, because
we know. So we stumble along without anyone's

help. And all the while we are overlooking the unsettled sense within, though if we paid attention to this we would see our true inner condition. In this way, we accustom our souls to straggling along in a spiritual wilderness, and we do ourselves harm.

Many, many are the Christian souls who are just like this. They do not know how to do anything other than to let their human senses guide them.

Then God intervenes. He arranges things so that, one day, all alone, there arises from within a sudden surprising awareness of their absolute emptiness. He may also bring them not only emptiness but an overwhelming sense of isolation from others, and of loss.

How few see this bleak moment for what it is—a chance to see their need for something that is beyond themselves. For their mind will never be able to erase the horror of coming to the edge of this bottomless chasm, which is a look down into the deadness of our own soul apart from the life of God. If you have ever come to this precipice, you know how quickly the soul wants to flee from itself and rushes to find something— anything at all—to "fill" itself again with noise and activity.

This is the moment, however, when it can cross over—from its own empty silence into an expectant quiet that is alive with His presence, from anxious restlessness into a calming stillness. Suddenly, the soul finds that within its dark chasm there is a secret well of water, springing up to overflowing with light and eternal life.

When you learn how to pass into this place in spirit, allow God to keep your soul in this refreshing silent tranquility. Your soul will fight Him, and will do so by trying to analyze what is happening and by creating mental images to capture in the memory this experience. All of this weighs down the soul, and pulls it back from walking in the spirit to walking in the understanding.

How silly and childish we are. We are like the little child whose mother knows what a long way they have to go, and so she tries to carry him in her arms. But he kicks and cries and demands to walk on his own. When the mother gives in and puts the child down, they make almost no progress at all because he is always stumbling, or hurting his foot, or distracted by this or that . . . until the joy of the walk is forgotten and he is peevish and miserable. . . .

Remember, when your soul discovers how to let the Holy Spirit bring it into this place of inner peace—*rest in this tranquility*. It is only because God is bearing you in His arms that you sense no work or movement on your part. This accomplishes far more than all of your own actions or works, since God is at work *in* you.

Allow your soul to remain in the hand of God, and to rest in confidence in Him alone. . . .

LIVING FLAME OF LOVE: STANZA 3

My Father, when I go about my days, forgetting you, forgetting it is you who gives me breath and life, remind me. Open my eyes to the fact that my life proceeds from you.

You are so kind to remain with me through every one of my days . . . as close to me as my heartbeat . . . and my every breath.

I ask for this gift: that I may remain simply, contentedly, close to you.

25
Hearing From the Lord

*T*he sinful mind is hostile to God. . . . Those
controlled by the sinful nature cannot please God.
You, however, are controlled not by the sinful nature
but by the Spirit, if the Spirit of God lives in you.

Romans 8:7–9

*S*amuel said [to the Lord], "Speak, for your servant
is listening."

1 Samuel 3:10

*S*ometimes, God chooses to reveal himself to
us by His Spirit in unusual ways. Sometimes He
may guide us by giving a mental image, or a
vision. Sometimes He moves by speaking to us
through supernatural *words*, and these may arise
from within ourselves, or come with startling
accuracy and insight from other spiritual people.

Though God *does* continue to speak this way

112

to us, there are several reasons why we must be careful about handling and interpreting the meanings of these special communications. We can trust God implicitly in His ability to speak— but we cannot, first of all, trust in our ability to hear Him accurately. Second, we forget that our sense of guidance from God is also subject to larger conditions around us. By that I mean God works on a grander scale, which affects not only the personal direction we feel we have been given, but when and how it will come about.

To begin with, our manner of thinking is not the same as God's. And until we start to adjust ourselves to His views and the way He speaks, it is truly as if we are two parties speaking different languages. We know, for instance, that a well-known saying in one culture makes no sense at all when translated into the language of another culture. And though God does accommodate himself in many ways to be able to communicate to us at all, when it comes to knowing His higher ways *we* must accommodate ourselves to Him.

Because God is so limitless, His eternal way of viewing the events that go on here below, in time, is vastly different from our own. So when He speaks to us, in visions and in special words of guidance, we must approach it carefully. For His ways, purposes, and viewpoints are so much higher—to speak plainly, *different* from ours.

In fact, you will see as you grow deeper in the Lord that His words and guidance to us often

113

show themselves to be most true and wonderful the more confusing and impossible they first appear.

Scripture shows us that this is a fact. For many of the people long ago, God's prophetic words did not come to pass in the way they expected. That was because, like us, they did not seek God's higher view first and interpreted what He told them from their own self-serving viewpoint—in the wrong way, that is. They also looked for absolutely literal fulfillments of God's word, ignoring the fact that He was addressing spiritual conditions.

In Genesis, for instance, God led Abraham to Canaan and said, "I will give you this land" (15:7). He repeated this promise to Abraham many times. Meanwhile, the years passed and Abraham grew older and older, and he never saw how in any way this land was his. So he asked, "Lord, how will this land be mine? Or what sign will you give me that this land is mine?"

Do you see? Abraham finally stirred himself above his limited viewpoint and asked for the Lord's mind in the matter. Then the Lord revealed to him that the land was not to be his personally, but that his sons—that is, his "sons" who would come 400 years later—would take possession of the land. Then Abraham understood. So God's work and promise was true after all, that out of love for Abraham God was giving him a gift.

If you think about Abraham's years of

confusion, you will see that he was deceived by the way he understood the prophecy. And if he had given up his faith in the Lord, or spoken of the Lord as unfaithful, he would have misled others as well. No one who was alive in Abraham's day was to see the promise fulfilled. If Abraham had told everyone the land would be *his*, and if he had held on to that belief, he would have gone to his grave an unhappy man, and those who heard his claims may have discredited him, his faith, and his God.

Likewise, when Jacob was summoned to Egypt by his son Joseph, he was traveling along the road when God spoke to him. "Jacob," He said, "do not be afraid to go down to Egypt, for I will be with you. And I will lead you out again."

If we looked on this matter in our way of seeing things, this promise was definitely *not* fulfilled. For the old man never left Egypt alive. But the word of the Lord was fulfilled generations later for the children of Jacob, when the Lord was their guide—quite literally and miraculously! Again, anyone who took God's promise to Jacob in literal and personal terms would have expected God to preserve the old man in health and vitality and bring him back to his former home. And he would have concluded, wrongly so, that God did not keep His word. . . .

As you can plainly see, receiving guidance and prophetic words from the Lord is a delicate matter. Many souls are easily deceived, because they hear what they want to hear. And others get caught up in the merely literal sense of it and do not comprehend the movements of the Spirit.

God's principal intent in speaking to us, however, is to convey the spirit of a matter. And in order to understand Him, we cannot leap to our own understanding, but must seek Him, and wait. . . . For the Spirit is living and full of meaning, far more than literal words themselves, and it has the miraculous ability to affect lives far beyond all we can imagine or expect. . . .

ASCENT OF MOUNT CARMEL: BOOK 2, CHAPTER 19

My Father, I have so far understood you in a certain way . . . but that is only sparsely, the way I understand a person who can barely speak my language. How foolish I have been . . .

. . . I need to learn, little by little, how to understand your language.

26
Dominion

In my vision at night I looked, and there before me
was one like a son of man,
coming with the clouds of heaven.
He approached the Ancient of Days
and was led into his presence.
He was given authority,
glory and sovereign power. . . .

Daniel 7:13–14

[Jesus said to the teacher of Israel],
"I have spoken to you of earthly things
and you do not believe;
how then will you believe
if I speak of heavenly things?"

John 3:12

God has far less interest in temporal
dominion and in temporal freedom. For in God's
eyes, neither one holds the *power* and *authority* of
true government or liberty at all. . . .

I want to be sure you understand this important principle: The Spirit and the eternal kingdom are first. So do not be deceived into interpreting the promises and instructions of our Lord without taking into account the full heights and depths of His Spirit. To try to limit His words only to what we can understand, and only to what is temporal, is small indeed. It is like attempting to grasp the air. Yes, you might succeed in snatching some small particle that is borne on the wind—but how can you trap the air itself in your hands? . . .

It is important for a man, if he is not truly spiritual, to comprehend how God is arranging and governing circumstances, or to understand how He works at all. . . . As the apostle Paul says, "The man without the Spirit does not accept the things that come from the Spirit of God, for they are foolishness to him. . . . The spiritual man makes judgments about all things" (1 Corinthians 2:14–15).

Let me give you a few examples so that you will more clearly understand. Suppose that a Christian man falls into the hand of enemies, who abuse and persecute him. He cries out to God, and God answers, saying, "I will set you free from all your enemies." This word may well be true, and yet his captors may continue in their own wickedness, and he may die at their hands.

Now if he or his friends expected God's

answer to come in terms of temporal freedom, they would have deceived themselves. For God may have meant that the man's deliverance would be that final, complete freedom—heaven, where there is full victory over this life. . . .

When God speaks, we must assume that He is referring first to the things that are most profitable and most important, and that is the life of the spirit. And if there is also a temporal meaning, we can trust Him to bring that to pass, too.

This is what we see in David's prophecy concerning Christ: "You will rule [the nations] with an iron scepter; you will dash them to pieces like pottery" (Psalm 2:9).

Here, God is speaking of that prime and perfect lordship of Christ, in which He will have a kingdom that is forever. In no way was this fulfilled by Christ on an earthly level, during His physical life. . . . For Christ was born in hard circumstances, lived in poverty, was betrayed, brutally beaten, and died a criminal's death in agony.

But in the eternal sense, the prophecy has been fulfilled. For Christ has been declared "a priest forever" (see Hebrews 7:17). And this came about because He submitted himself fully to God, soul and body, and allowed the Father to fulfill His promises just as He saw fit. . . .

Think carefully on this: God is like a spring, and from Him everyone draws water according to the type of vessel he carries.

Remember that God told Samuel to listen to the outcry of the people who were demanding a king. For in their demand to have what every other nation had—a human king—they were rejecting God's reign over them (see 1 Samuel 8:6–8). In this same way, God stoops to some souls and gives them what they demand, even though it is not best for them, because they are either headstrong or weak. They will not rest at peace in His hand so that He can easily direct them.

You may have wondered why some souls always pray for and always receive only tender and sweet things. God grants them these things because they cannot, or will not, receive anything else from His hands.

He would prefer they partake of stronger food—that is, the way of the cross, accepting trials, which purify. . . .

ASCENT OF MOUNT CARMEL: BOOK 2, CHAPTERS 19 AND !

My Eternal Father, I am grateful that you do fulfill your promises, and you do answer my prayers, sometimes in wonderful and surprising ways.

Help me also to be grateful when your answer is

not to my liking . . . because you are laying deeper foundations for the purposes of your kingdom . . . because you want to set in me the cornerstone of Christlikeness.

27
The Word of the Lord

Seek the Lord while he may be found. . . .

Isaiah 55:6

And the Lord said [to the prophet Micaiah], "These people have no master. . . ." "So now the Lord has put a lying spirit in the mouths of all these prophets of yours. . . ."

1 Kings 22:17, 23

---

*[Jesus] . . . said unto them,
"An evil and adulterous generation
seeketh after a sign; and
there shall no sign be given to it,
but the sign of the prophet Jonas . . .
so shall the Son of man be three days and three nights
in the heart of the earth."*

Matthew 12:39–40, KJV

Because the devil has such great powers to ensnare, we must beware at all times. For at the moment we forget our low estate and think we have become spiritual and specially gifted, we have become wrong-spirited and we are in grave danger. This is a serious warning to those who have experienced special inner guidance and spiritual gifts. Do not slip from your place in Christ on the misstep of hidden pride.

It is true that Scripture encourages us to seek spiritual gifts (see 1 Corinthians 14:1). For a vessel to contain purest water, though, it must surely be cleansed. And it must be cleansed again tomorrow, and cleansed each day thereafter, in order to remain clean. Otherwise, the water it contains will not be clean and pure.

Many have gone astray on this path. In the first place, they have not learned to walk in the Spirit—which is pleasing to God—in the attitude of Christ, who sought no power of His own, no reputation of His own (see Philippians 2). If you do not have this attitude, this mind of Christ, in you, then you have no part with Christ. For if you only believe the doctrines of Christianity with your mind, while your natural inner man secretly hates the ways of God, you are at the headwaters of a stream that issues many, many evils.

I am referring to the wellspring of *pride*. Remember that pride is not just an attitude of superiority, it is the subtle desire, always present, to be free from a moment-by-moment dependence upon God. This is the root of all vainglory. If you do not recognize it and be on constant guard against this independent attitude, you will forget that you are always to *seek the Lord first*.

If we move away from constant dependence upon Him, then our motive for seeking to experience a spiritual gift can be poisoned with tinctures of evil. The first is the evil of *presumption*—that is, presuming we can have spiritual power or insight that is especially our own, and which can be used and directed as we desire (see Acts 8:9–24). Another is the evil of seeking spiritual gifts because we are merely bored and *curious*—which is often a sign that our roots are not in the Lord and so we are spiritually dry and dissatisfied.

Do you see my point? Anything that springs from our soul's incessant desire to remain independent from the humble Spirit of Christ—which is abasement—leads us into tremendous peril. . . .

To wander off the sure path—which is total trust and abandonment to the love of God—carries you away from living in Him. If you wander out from the Spirit of Christ, you have found your way back to the outer darkness, the path of your own determination. Many who have done so wonder why they have experienced spiritual giftings, and yet inwardly they feel opposition and no peace. It is as if they were unbelievers again, under God's wrath.

I tell you, it *is* God's rod of wrath, driving them back into the humble, simple way He first called them to walk. For in His greater love, He will purposely allow us to go farther and farther astray—especially when we insist on being so spiritually sure of ourselves that we become blind. When we leave His ordered and safe paths, He will give free rein to our vain seeking after glory and to our wild imaginings.

For this reason, God warned us through the prophet Isaiah. He said that He would chasten and correct those who seek after signs and spiritual experiences with a spirit of dissension, confusion, and dizziness (see Isaiah 19:14). . . . So we can see that, although God will always answer us, His children, He sometimes complains. . . . For God does not want us to seek special guidance and visions first. Those He gives when He wills. First, He wants us to seek Him.

ASCENT OF MOUNT CARMEL: BOOK 2, CHAPTER 21

My Father, you have spoken your first and greatest Word to me. His name is Jesus.

Before I seek any other word or sign from you, I will let you search my heart to see that it is clean and willing to follow you in humility . . . no matter what.

28
Refreshed

I have become in [my Lover's] eyes like one bringing contentment . . . as one that has found favor.

Song of Songs 8:10, (last phrase, KJV)

Whom shall [the Lord] teach knowledge? and whom shall he make to understand doctrine? To whom he said, [This spiritual perception and judgment] is the rest wherewith ye may cause the weary to rest; and this is the refreshing. . . ."

Isaiah 28:9, 12, KJV

When it is necessary, wrench your soul free from its thirst and hunger for lower things—from inner thrills and delights. This will not do you a bit of harm, and in fact it will help you to make great spiritual progress.

As the prophet Habakkuk said: "O Lord, are you not from everlasting? I will stand at my watch and station myself on the ramparts; I will look to see what he will say to me . . ." (1:12; 2:1).

This means, I will leave below what my senses tell me—all those fear-filled thoughts that have formed walls behind which my soul hides from the Lord and will not trust itself to go out to Him. The prophet tells me to climb up and stand on top of these walls—that is, to rise above the soul and receive only what the Lord will give to me.

For if you want to receive anything from God you must open to Him entirely. And it is not possible for a soul to receive into itself the lofty One, who is Wisdom and Light from above, unless it has quieted the noise of its fleshly thinking and soulish crying.

Fight to withdraw your soul from this infancy. No, it is worse than infancy—it is a yoke of slavery around your neck, holding you captive in your own personal, spiritual Egypt. . . .

When your soul is restless, needing to be directed aright, I *plead* with you: Send it fleeing into the silent "wilderness" with God. There it will find the freedom and holy rest that are the heritage of the true sons of God. . . .

"Labor to get into this rest" (Hebrews 4:11). You labor by forcefully detaching the soul as it whines for constant assurances and spiritual comforts. Do not allow even a single troubling thought to enter your head, such as: "If I were truly a spiritual person, would I not feel spiritual? Would other people not remark about the signs and evidences of my spiritual growth?" . . .

When you pray, make no provision at all for

the flesh: Allow only an inner state of full tranquility to come. That is how the emptied and cleansed vessel of your soul will be abundantly flooded with the Holy Spirit. That is how you will be penetrated to the depths by God's pure Light.

Then you will know the compassionate, satisfying, peace-giver, the One who is your all in all . . . the Lover of your soul, who is above all other loves. . . .

LIVING FLAME OF LOVE: STANZA 3

My Father—highest One! The voice of the world, and my own soul, would bind me to my feelings. These voices tell me, "You have a right to be angry," or "You should be sad, considering what's happened to you."

Father, you sent Jesus to be both Son of Man and Son of God. So I know that you can teach me how to be fully human . . . and also, by your Spirit, to live above my fallen humanity.

29
Satisfied

*The children of Israel journeyed from the
wilderness. . . . And the people thirsted there for
water. . . . And the Lord said unto Moses. . . .
"Behold, I will stand before thee there upon the rock
. . . and there shall come water out of it. . . ."*

Exodus 17:1, 3, 5–6, KJV

Some recoil at the spiritual path I have
described for you—that is, the way of
detachment from our thoughts and feelings that
leave us spiritually thirsty. They object, saying,
"Isn't it unnatural to simply ignore your feelings
and your own will?"

Not at all. For we rise above everything that
blinds the eyes of the soul, by passing beyond the
dark night of the soul. We press on and find God
by seeking Him in the time of absolute dryness,
when nothing satisfies the inner man's thirst.

Only as we achieve some distance from our
soul's thirsts and demands can we gain any
understanding of the selfishness that motivates

all we do—even our seeking of God. This is why St. Augustine said to God, "Let me know myself, Lord. And then I will know you." For as the philosophers say, one extreme is known by the other.

Do you understand this? We must know our inner selves in order to distinguish our own voice from the true voice of God. We must know our secret selfish motives, so that we can set them aside and begin to move in the eternal purposes of God.

David was a friend of God, and God led him through this same dark night and this dryness. He did this to show David the soul's only way to reach the higher knowledge of God, and to walk in His strength. . . .

David describes a wondrous event, really, when he tells of this transformation from a fleshly man to a spiritual man. This occurred when all the joy and pleasure—the wellsprings of his inner being—dried up completely. He found himself spiritually empty and alone, in an arid place. In his utter desolation, his mind could no longer help him, for even the mental pictures of God he had once conceived were not enough. Without any familiar "hold," his inner being was left to wander as in a pathless, waterless place.

That is how David describes the moment when he became aware—for the first time perhaps—that everything he knew of God was limited by his own comprehension. For every one of us, this is limited indeed. How can any human mind conceive the transcendent God who inhabits eternity? (see Isaiah 57:15).

Each of us must realize, like David, that even our highest thoughts are utterly low: This is how God brings to life in us a *humble spirit*. For it must dawn upon us that we know nothing at all, and only then are we open to drink from His Spirit. This type of humility must come, to replace our spiritual pride.

Do not resist. Let the Lord himself lead you to the place where you see exactly how dry and miserable you are apart from Him.

DARK NIGHT OF THE SOUL: BOOK 1, CHAPTER 7

My Father—Rock of my salvation, when I think I am walking in the light of understanding, help me to be sure the Light is you.

When I am walking in darkness, on shifting ground, remind me that you are still leading me by the hand . . . no matter that I cannot feel your touch. Remind me when I am passing through even the driest place that you are ahead of me, opening secret springs of water for my soul.

30
Shadow of God

*The Lord reigns, let the earth be glad. . . . Clouds
and thick darkness surround him. . . .*

———

Psalm 97:1–2

*He who dwells in the shelter of the Most High will
rest in the shadow of the Almighty.*

———

Psalm 91:1

.

God takes time to prepare the soul that He
wants to lead onward, with patience and
gentleness. His Majesty allows us years to
accustom ourselves to the spiritual life in general,
and that is because of the limitless forbearance
and kindness that flow from His vast love.

Yes, as we first begin our deeper walk in the
Spirit, He will indeed lead us through intense
trials of faith and emptiness, which feel like
traveling through a spiritual wilderness. As you
come out of such a time, you will feel as if you
have been purged. You will find yourself in a

place of great peace. It is as if you have made a breakthrough and escaped from a hard imprisonment into an open land of running springs.

The soul feels as if a new well has been opened up within it. Up from this new stream of God's Spirit, there flows a sense of greater freedom from the circumstances of life, which used to control and trouble the soul. The soul no longer has to work itself up with "spiritual thoughts," in order to find this place of inner rest. For the waters of this stream continually flow without any help or effort by us at all. They are always flowing up from within to soothe the soul whenever it becomes fretful, distracted, or anxious.

In another way of speaking, it is as if the soul has climbed to a higher place, a place of serene rest. And from this new height, it can look down and examine both the earthly things that would attack its peace *and* its own inner weaknesses, which make it subject to attack.

So the soul experiences far more freedom and happiness than it did in the beginning, before it learned how to rise above the dark night of its natural senses and earthbound ways of thinking.

As I have said, God allows us time to become stronger and more proficient in our ability to walk this way, in the Spirit.

Others may notice striking changes in you—a new kind of light and purity coming from inside.

And even this is only a beginning. It is like the hopeful radiance of a bride who is preparing for union with her Lover. To think—this is the same Light that shines upon those who have already passed into the untellable joy of heaven. And it shines upon those of us here below, who are still being made ready.

And now, if God so chooses, the soul may be led at some later time through another kind of "dark night." This is not the same as before, a quieting of its lower thoughts and base emotions. In this night, the soul may encounter the torment and deadness of despair. It may feel itself abandoned to the terrors of the night—that is, it may feel itself slipping into the open mouth of spiritual death itself.

How could God be part of such a thing? Why would He allow the soul to suffer in this way?

The first thing I will show you, in answer to this, is *the fluency of God's Wisdom*. For it is so much higher than our own, and is of an altogether different quality. When this Spirit of Wisdom comes we cannot miss the sharp distinctions: The Wisdom of God is swift, clear, without taint, irresistible, full of benevolence, compassionate and humane, steadfast and sure, freeing from anxiety, all-powerful, with gentle care it oversees all things.

This is the Spirit who works to penetrate and suffuse all spirits that are open to the intelligence of God, pure in their desire to see Him become all

135

in all. It is the breath of God, the might of His Spirit—the purest emanation of the glory of the Almighty.

As this eternal light approaches, you may easily understand how the soul—no matter how far it has progressed—will begin to perceive its utter insignificance. So there arises the sense of vileness, the overwhelming darkness of despair.

It will help you to understand this, as I refer to the wisdom of the ancients. They knew that the more clear and pure the divine things are that God wants to show us, the darker and more hidden they appear at first. This makes sense if you consider the sun: The brighter it shines, the more it overwhelms and blinds the eye—for the eye is too weak to take in such brightness. In the same way, the divine light that prepares us for greater union with God overwhelms the soul with "darkness." And for a time, the soul is pitched into a terrible state, because God, in His greater intelligence, is coming closer to the far lesser intelligence of the human soul. . . .

David has told us that the nearer God comes to us, the greater are the clouds and darkness that overtake us before His presence is revealed. Not that God himself is dark (see 1 John 1:5). But surely you must see that, weak in our own understanding, we must first be blinded and darkened by so tremendous a light. . . .

And this is what will occur if God chooses to send out from himself this ray of Wisdom, in

order to lift and transform us, and to make us
closer to Him. . . .

DARK NIGHT OF THE SOUL: BOOK 2, CHAPTER 5

*My Comforting Father, everything
within me resists the thought that you are Lord over all
. . . even depression and despair.*

*When I am desolate, I will lift my sights above my
poor condition . . . and wait for a new light to fall
within me . . . serene . . . bringing "colors" beyond
the spectrum of earth's colors . . . showing me a new
shade called hope.*

31
Love Everlasting

The Lord appeared . . . saying, "I have loved you
with an everlasting love. . . . I will make an
everlasting covenant with [you]. . . . I will rejoice in
doing [you] good. . . . For the Lord will be your
everlasting light."

———

Jeremiah 31:3; 32:40–41; Isaiah 60:19

When Moses was on Mount Sinai, God
passed before him. So magnificent and
overwhelming was the presence of God that
Moses threw himself face down on the ground.

What passed before Moses might be described
as the bright gleaming facets of God's nature, His
invisible qualities. The sight was so brilliant that
Moses was stunned. And later, when he was
given the plan for the tabernacle and the holy
place, these eternal brightnesses were presented
by the ever-burning "lamps."

On Sinai, though, as the Lord passed, He
proclaimed His brilliant attributes: *The Lord, the*
Lord, the compassionate and gracious God, slow to

anger, abounding in love and faithfulness, maintaining love to thousands, and forgiving wickedness, rebellion and sin . . . (Exodus 34:6–7).

These are the aspects of God himself, which struck Moses' heart so that he loved and knew God more profoundly than even before.

This is the way in which God shines His Light—which contains many lights—into our soul. For His Light is all of His many virtues, and when He allows these to burn within us, we know He has "revealed" himself. Though we do not see Him with our eyes, we say He has "shown" himself within our soul, when the lights of His glory pass within us.

Is it any wonder that the soul feels it is being lifted and opened, rising as if on a current of pure and wordless joy, whenever He is near? . . . The soul is completely absorbed . . . and we know beyond human knowing that His love is Life. We long for the day when we are united with Him in eternity and we are filled forever with this Love and this Life.

A soul must experience this touch of God, when His lights actually pass within—and then the words of Solomon's *Song of Songs*, the tender words of those two lovers, will be illuminated with true knowing. . . .

Not only will you understand the attributes of God himself, as I say, but a greater thing will come to pass as well. He is planting His "seeds of fire," His attributes within you as He passes. And you may be sure that He will protect and nurture this seed, for He fully intends that His character be reproduced in you.

For when you love another person, you do good to him—and you do good to him according to the best that is in your own nature. Therefore, consider these things:

Since your soul's Spouse, who walks and lives within you, is *omnipotent*, He gives you omnipotence as He loves you with all His might! And since He is *Wisdom*, you perceive that He is loving you in the highest and best ways— knowing His ways are above those of mere men. Since He is *holy*, He loves you with a love that is at work to set you apart for himself. Since He is *righteous*, He will love you in a way that leads you in His paths of righteousness.

And more—He that loves you is *merciful, compassionate, meek*. He is altogether *strong, sublime*, and *delicate*. He is a Lover who is *clean, pure*, and *forever true*. He loves you *liberally, without self-interest*, and with every intention to do *good* to you.

The One who loves you is *humility* itself. He thinks of you and cares for you with the highest esteem. He even makes himself your equal, and joyfully shows you every expression of His grace.

This One who revealed himself to Moses says to you: "I am yours. I am *for* you. It gives me the greatest delight to bring all that is in my name—I

AM—and give it all to you. My desire is to be yours."

How can anyone give words to the sheer delight of knowing you are so loved, so lifted up by the Lover, and held in such tender esteem?

LIVING FLAME OF LOVE: STANZA 3

My Majestic Father—knowing this is a bold prayer . . . knowing you have told me to come boldly before your throne to seek you . . .

I ask that you show me your glory, so that what is prideful in me will be driven to its knees . . . worshiping in the light of you.

32

Fortress of Light

*How great is your goodness . . . which you bestow
. . . on those who take refuge in you. . . . [The Lord]
showed his wonderful love to me. . . . Be strong and
take heart, all you who hope in the Lord. . . .*

Psalm 31:19, 21, 24

*The Lord's unfailing love surrounds the man who
trusts in him.*

Psalm 32:10

The serene peace and spiritual sweetness that
the Lord gives is not the type of inner peace for
which we normally hunger.

We want a peace that merely comforts and
coddles, because we do not like to be challenged
or changed. And so we make the mistake of
thinking we have peace, when really we are
receiving comfort—temporal and temporary as it
is—from our strong hold on the security and
assurance that comes only from without.

The peace that flows into us from the Lord satisfies the soul with full assurance that He is still *for* us, even as we are being taken through fire—in which we can be changed into His likeness. . . .

I have said much to you about the blinding power of human thinking and perceptions—all that darkens the eyes of the soul. This includes the insistence that you feel something every time you seek God's presence, as "proof" that He has really come to you. . . .

And I have told you that God sends dryness to wean you from feelings and comforts, so that you may grow and become mature. May you soon understand what it means to live above the soul's demands, and never again to allow them to dictate to you in matters of the spirit. The soul's former hungers wane and the old attachments will lose their hold, just as when an infant stops nursing, the courses of the mother's milk run dry. . . .

As we allow Him to take from us what we no longer need, we receive a spiritual strength of incomparable benefit: Whether we are experiencing loss or gain, weakness or strength— everything in our life reminds us to praise and thank God for His unfailing presence. For now we clearly see our own demands for what they are, attempts to shape our life, and others' too, in *our* image. No matter how strong and in control this makes us feel, it is *deadness* and *darkness* itself.

Now we can receive *all* as coming from God. Every event—whether it affects us without or within—all of it is another reminding touch from the Master's hand. And He is such a good Sovereign that He is able to use everything to call to us without words. This is what He wants— that the world should lose its power over us, as we draw into Him—into the great Love that is God himself.

This is how we grow in spiritual vision and hunger for God alone—if we learn to see that every challenge offers us great benefit if it causes us to flee into God. Others have called this *fortitude*.

The virtue of fortitude is often mistaken as merely drawing strength from God. But then we believe we have strength in ourselves, and there is nothing so weak and failing as that. Fortitude comes upon us when the soul has found its one unfailing shelter—that is, when we have seen with the eyes of faith how our soul has fled into its all-surrounding God. He alone is our everlasting wall of strength. . . .

DARK NIGHT OF THE SOUL: BOOK 1, CHAPTER 13

My Father, as you begin to open new eyes of faith in me, I am starting to see that you are my soul's true Fortress. I can see that everything you allow to be taken from me is taken, not to harm me, but that I may know what it means to be "hidden with Christ" in you. . . .

In this moment, let me know your mighty, surrounding power!

33
Dawn of Wisdom

*As King David approached Bahurim . . . Shimei . . .
cursed as he came out. He pelted David [with stones]
. . . Abishai son of Zeruiah said to the king, "Why
should this dead dog curse my lord, the king? Let me
go over and cut off his head." But [David] said,
"What do you and I have in common. . . ? If he is
cursing because the Lord said to him, 'Curse David,'
who can ask, 'Why do you do this?' "*

2 Samuel 16:5–6, 9–10

*The fear of the Lord is the beginning of wisdom, and
knowledge of the Holy One is understanding.*

Proverbs 9:10

There are times when the soul goes through
humbling experiences. Formerly, there was
strength, calm, security, confidence. Then all that
is stripped, and the soul sees itself in its true
state of desperate need. If we are alert, we
recognize that the Lord is opening our eyes to

146

secret pride—the thinking that all our achievements are of ourselves and not purely a gift from above.

Yes, these times come so it will never occur to us again that we are stronger in spirit than anyone else. For if we look upon any other person as weaker, it is only because we have not been taken through the purging fire of God. Perhaps this is what is happening to them, and it is no business of ours. On the contrary, God means for us to have an open and humble spirit, realizing that, in their position, we may not handle the circumstances as well—and might do worse.

I want you to see that this humbling process is in God's hands. It is His way of raising in your heart a new love for all men. In the past, you may have judged them—either for their pride, or for being in personal difficulties. Worse, you have seen others who are lukewarm or weak in their faith and compared it with your own strong devotion and enthusiasm for God.

As I say, God has His ways of changing such a high-minded attitude. God is merciful, who shows us all our own wretched emptiness—this is how He knocks us out of the seat of judgment, which is His seat alone. He wants us to keep our eyes on our own response to what we know He wants us to do, so that we remain in a state of simple obedience to Him.

David stood in the presence of wicked men,

wondering why the Lord tolerated their evil behavior while he went through such anguish in his own life. Nevertheless, he prayed, "I will watch *my* ways and keep my tongue from sin . . ." (Psalm 39:1). And when he saw how small and limited was his own viewpoint, he continued, saying, "I was silent; I would not open my mouth, for you are the one who has done this" (v. 9).

This is the humble condition to which the Lord will bring your soul if you are on the spiritual road. He longs to help you be submitted to His hand alone, obedient to His voice alone. We are not at rest in Him if we are looking about to see how He is dealing with others. Nor are we at His service to bring the grace of compassion to them, if we have taken a higher seat.

In this way, our heart becomes tender to the voice of the Lord, listening for what He will say, no matter who He allows to bring the message. Before, in our arrogance, we would only receive teaching and correction from someone we thought worthy. Now our ears are opened to His voice alone. And we may enjoy the benefit of knowing we are always under the sovereign direction of the Lord.

Remember that He may use anyone at all—however unwitting they may be—to teach us and direct us on our way.

DARK NIGHT OF THE SOUL: CHAPTER 12

My Father, you have sent certain people into my life . . . who irritate, and even make me feel degraded. Thank you that you allow me to set a distance between them and me, so that I can find quiet sacred space again . . . to let you speak . . .

Remind me every day that, hidden in you, no evil word spoken against me has any power . . . and no vicious action directed at me is "deserved."

Free me to receive my deepest needs from you first and last.

34
The Father's Table

Your love, O Lord, reaches to the heavens, your faithfulness to the skies. . . . How priceless is your unfailing love! Both high and low among men find refuge in the shadow of your wings. They feast on the abundance of your house; you give them drink from your river of delights. For with you is the fountain of life; in your light we see light.

Psalm 36:5, 7–9

God gives to each one of us exactly what we need, and He gives it in the way we need to receive it. . . .

The father of a family will see to it that his table is laden with many kinds of food, some of which is better and more nutritious than others. One of his children wants to eat only a certain dish and, as it happens, this is not the best food for him. But it is the one he would rather eat. How well the father knows this particular child! If he serves the better dish, he knows the child will only push his plate away and refuse to eat at all, since he will only eat his favorite food.

Therefore, rather than let the foolish and demanding and beloved child go hungry, the father may, with regret, give it the food that is pleasing—all the while wishing the child would grow up and develop a taste for better things.

ASCENT OF MOUNT CARMEL: BOOK 2, CHAPTER 21

My Father, I praise you, that you welcome me at your table. It's true I would rather not accept some of the things you pass my way.

But today, I will happily sit at the place you have set for me . . . enjoying the joy . . . being your child.

35
Highest Word

*My purpose is that . . . [you] may have the full
riches of complete understanding, in order that [you]
may know the mystery of God, namely, Christ, in
whom are hidden all the treasures of wisdom
and knowledge.*

———

Colossians 2:2–3

*In the past God spoke to our forefathers through the
prophets at many times and in various ways, but in
these last days he has spoken to us by his Son, whom
he appointed heir of all things, and through whom he
made the universe. The Son is the radiance of the
Father's glory and the exact representation
of his being. . . .*

———

Hebrews 1:1–3

Our faith must be firmly built on the
foundation of Christ himself. This is the era of
grace and the gospel—that is the way God has
chosen to bring our souls under His good

rulership. It has not only been spoken to us, it has been lived out before human eyes. . . .

Jesus, God's Son, is His living Word—He has no other. Having spoken His true message to us altogether in this one Word, once and for all, He has no reason to speak anything that would replace this Word. . . .

Therefore, if anyone seeks God, asking Him for a vision or revelation of some so-called "higher truth," he must beware that he is not acting foolishly, possibly committing an offense against God. Far better that this man learn what it means to fix his eyes upon Christ—to see the utter humility, love, and obedience revealed in His life.

Take care! When you seek some new "word" from God—a new method or means to live the spiritual life—you are in danger of pushing aside the one perfect Word that He has given us already. It is as if we are saying to God that this Word is not enough to satisfy.

Perhaps God is speaking to you now, saying:

"If I have spoken all things to you in my Word, which is my Son, and I have no other Word to say to you—what other answer can I give you? what 'higher' revelation than His very Life, which is your Way to ascend to me?

"Fix your eyes on Him alone, for in Him I have spoken and shown you everything. If you live in Him, you will find more than you could ever ask or even imagine (see Ephesians 3:20).

"You ask for special guidance, answers to prayers, which are the smaller part—the least of what I would give you. If you fix your eyes upon Christ, I will give you *all*. For He is my complete Word and answer for you. He is the fullness of my goal and ambition, hidden for so long and now openly revealed to you (see Ephesians 3:7–12).

"Do you not understand that I have already spoken to you, even before you seek me or pray? I have already answered you . . . in giving Jesus to you as your brother, companion, master. He is your ransom and your prize. . . .

"If you seek me for answers when you are in need of comfort and consolation, consider my Son—subject to me in all things, bound by His love of me, and afflicted—and you will understand how fully He is your answer.

"If you seek me for deeper spiritual knowledge, set your eyes on Him—and you will find the rarest treasures opened to you, all the wisdom and wonders of God, which are hidden in Christ (see Colossians 2:3).

"Nothing that you seek can be as satisfying to your soul, no other answer as beneficial, as seeing Christ with the eyes and understanding of your inner man. For as my apostle, Paul, said, 'I resolved to know nothing . . . except Jesus Christ and him crucified' " (1 Corinthians 2:2).

In all things, see that you are guided by the "law" of Christ made man . . . He himself is our

154

means to remedy our spiritual weakness and ignorance.

For by living in Christ, we find abundant "medicine" for all our spiritual ailments. . . . Nothing, not even so-called supernatural revelations, can replace the one and greatest Word. . . .

ASCENT OF MOUNT CARMEL: BOOK 2, CHAPTER 22

My Father, still my heart. Tune my ear. Teach me what I need to know today from your most perfect Word . . . Jesus.

36
Rising Sun

Who is this that appears . . . bright as the sun. . . ?

Song of Songs 6:10

In the heavens [God] has pitched a tent for the sun,
which is a bridegroom coming forth from his pavilion,
like a champion rejoicing. . . .

Psalm 19:4–5

*B*efore the soul discovers what is meant by
the precious union with God, it is in darkness.

True, you may have knowledge of the
Scriptures, and may have mental agreement with
the doctrines of Christ. But until God speaks—
"Let there be light!"—a thick darkness covers the
abyss of every soul. . . .

It is not possible for the soul to lift its eyes to
the true Light of God. Nor can it conceive what
this Light is, or how it will come. . . . Therefore,
when we say we want God to give us His light,
what we really mean is that we want more of

natural understanding—we want to be able to grasp His ways, usually in order to decide on our own what God will and will not call us to do. . . .

But "deep calls to deep" (Psalm 42:7). And God can only be described, in all His vast array of glories, as a splendid "chasm" of endless light. And it is this endless Light that calls to the dark depths of our being. For His Light must infuse our darkness—there can be no other way for what is of darkness, at last, to know Light. . . .

The soul that journeys in God will come to see how blind it has always been, taking pleasure in anything other than God. It is as if a cloud covers the eye of spiritual understanding, so that, in acting according to its rational senses alone, it has been acting insanely. . . .

I pray you will come to see how puny are the "great matters" on which you continually fix your eyes. In fact, it is as if you persist in setting a tiny, useless object on the end of your nose. It cannot help but obstruct the vast and spectacular vista that would actually lift your soul—an eternal horizon shot with color, wonder, and indescribable light!

Consider this, when you are tempted to let some small desire or useless purpose draw your sight from God, and from the rising of His great Light, and from its penetrating rays. . . .

LIVING FLAME OF LOVE: STANZA 3

Father of depth, beauty and wonder, why do I hold out till the last, clutching at something I see as big and important . . . when it is so small and insignificant?

Please, Father, remove from me one more of those small obstructions . . . the one that blocks from my view the particular aspect of your wonder that I most need to see . . . one more ray of your rising sun.

37
Flame, Holy Spirit!

*But when the Comforter is come, whom [Jesus] will
send unto you from the Father, even the Spirit of
truth, which proceedeth from the Father,
he shall testify of me.*

John 15:26, KJV

*The Spirit helps us in our weakness. We do not know
what we ought to pray for, but the Spirit himself
intercedes for us with groans that words cannot
express. And he who searches our hearts knows the
mind of the Spirit, because the Spirit intercedes for the
saints in accordance with God's will.*

Romans 8:26–27

Oh, Holy Spirit . . .

Oh, Fire! that so intimately and tenderly
penetrates the fibre and core of my soul. . . .
Cleanse me, burn in me, with your passion for
Christ!

You are so kind and loving to show me that

your one desire is to give yourself to me in life eternal. Forgive me if the things I used to ask for were so senseless, for my prayers were coming as from a blind man. In my soul's weakness, I yearn for so many things that my love for you grows weak. . . . Forgive me the times when, in my secret heart, I have wanted you to let me go. Forgive me for my impatience, when all the while you are forming the very conditions that surround me, so that you can mold me into the image that is of your making.

In times past, I have felt a certain kind of love for you rising up in me—only to have it weaken and die. I know that love was of the wrong "substance," for it was driven only by weak motives. *I wanted your comforts and blessings, and not you alone!*

Now I come before you only to ask this: Whatever you desire for me, mold me and make me to desire the same thing. Whatever you do not want for me, tear it from my heart—do not allow even the thought of it to pass through my mind.

Now I see that my truest prayers are not of myself. They are born in the Father's heart, they proceed from Him to me, carried by your hand, Holy Spirit. And they pour through my innermost being, flooding me with a crushing joy. And the discernment I now have comes from fixing my eyes upon your face, to read your slightest change of expression, so that I know what is meant for me and what is not. In this way you have lifted my prayers.

When your Spirit is upon me, in me, I could ask for you to break the slender web of this life—I can scarcely wait for age and years to let me go into your presence! For I long for that day when I can love you, fully, with greatest satisfaction, without end and forever. . . .

No matter what my soul may try to tell me at other times, this perfect union with you is my one desire.

LIVING FLAME OF LOVE: STANZA 2

38
God's Dwelling Place

We speak of God's secret wisdom, a wisdom that has been hidden and that God destined for our glory before time began. . . .

1 Corinthians 2:7

You yourselves are God's temple . . . and God's Spirit lives in you.

1 Corinthians 3:16

I must tell you one of the greatest wonders of God:

The flame of His presence is so intense it could devour a thousand worlds, the way natural fire kindles a fragile thread of flax. Yet this same consuming fire falls upon us. Though it consumes our darkness, it wreaks no destruction at all on the soul itself. In us it comes tender to rest.

Let Him come tenderly! Allow His flame within—it will not destroy you, but give you unspeakable joy as it issues the grace and godliness in you. And the more He purifies, the more beautifully His brightness burns.

In the Book of *Acts* we read that when the fire of the Holy Spirit fell on the disciples, it came roaring upon them with great vehemence (see Acts 2). As Gregory tells us, God burns inwardly with sweetness.

By the Holy Spirit—this is how God communicates himself to us. And not only once, but many, many times. For God is at work to enlarge the capacity of the soul, which is His temple. He must create this holy space within us little by little. For in our poor, weak condition we cannot stand to be enlarged by the coming of His presence all at once. If He were to come upon us in His fullness, the soul could not stand the explosive might of His great glory.

And so He delights us, bathing our souls in the light of His glory and richness. This is the sweetness for which every soul longs.

Happy are you indeed, when the fire of God kindles in its sanctuary inside you—and you do not shrink or hold back from its cleansing glory!

This is the transformation: You will be so at rest in the hand of God that He will be able to teach you anything He desires, knowing that you will not complain, resist or argue. You will grow rich—that is, *rich in the presence of God!*

Nothing will prevail against your soul.
Nothing will be able to touch you!

So this is the marvel: God's slightest touch
could utterly annihilate—yet His only desire is to
embrace us, with a love that knows no limits at
all. . . .

Never doubt that this is God's will for you.
Never doubt that He is *able* to lift your soul to so
high a state.

LIVING FLAME OF LOVE: STANZA 2

*My Tender Father, I want . . . I need
. . . to be flooded with the love that comes from you.*

*I rejoice in the wonder of knowing this: Your
presence . . . which holds the terrifying power to create
worlds and destroy evil . . . is here to embrace me right
now.*

39
Celebration

The son said to him, "Father, I have sinned against heaven and against you. I am no longer worthy to be called your son." But the father said to his servants, "Quick! Bring the best robe and put it on him. Put a ring on his finger. . . . For this son of mine was dead and is alive again. . . ." So they began to celebrate.

Luke 15:21–22, 24

*T*he King of heaven has been longing to show himself to you.

He has come down from His lofty position, to show that He wants to walk alongside you. He has even become a man, so you will know He is your friend.

Think deeply on these things, for you must grasp the height and depth of what His coming means. Then you will no longer have a cringing fear of Him, like a miserable slave. You will know that He has no wrath toward you, but that His heart is inclined toward you with a gentle kindness. He will be able to show you the full strength of His might, and you will know that, in love, He only uses it for your goodness.

You have been longing, perhaps, to know that you can lean back against His breast . . . without fear . . . and like a close friend. I am telling you, you can. From the day that He came to establish His throne in your soul, His one desire is to meet you, the way a bridegroom is eager to come out from His hidden chambers for the one He loves.

God leans into your soul. He reaches out with His hand, and it is as if we have been graced with the touch of a scepter. He wants only to embrace you as a brother—for you were lost and are now on your way home.

Yes, He has come out to meet you, carrying royal vesture. You smell its fragrance—which are all the virtues of God with which He wants to clothe you. In amazement, you see its golden splendor—which is nothing less than the shining love of God. . . .

All of this is done *to* you, *for* you, and *in* you. And you know that you are being changed. Your spirit is being robed in the garment of spiritual strength that is sent especially for you by no one less than the King of heaven! . . .

Know then—with a certainty past all feeling— that the King dwells secretly in you. He holds you, and will not let you go away from Him again.

LIVING FLAME OF LOVE: STANZA 4

My Father, King of Heaven!—never let me wander far from you again. When blessing fills my days with simple happiness . . . let me know it is the fragrance of your goodness as you walk near me.

I worship you . . . adore you. . . .

40
His Coming

O Lord my God, you are very great; you are clothed
with splendor and majesty. He wraps himself with
light as with a garment. . . . He makes the clouds his
chariot and rides on the wings of the wind. . . . When
you send your Spirit . . . you renew. . . .

Psalm 104:1–3, 30

[Jesus] says, "Yes, I am coming soon."

Revelation 22:20

*E*ternal and everlasting Father, you, who hold
the power of death and life, no one can run from
your hand.

You, who are life eternal, you never kill except
to raise us to new life. You never wound except to
heal.

You have wounded me with your loving hand,
in order to make me well. You have killed in me
the very thing that would have killed me. The life
that I now see in me is the life of God (see
Galatians 2:20).

168

This is what you have set out to accomplish in all of us, your children. You work by lavishly pouring on us your unceasing streams of grace. You touch us by showing us the downcast beauty, and the uplifted majesty that is in the face of your only begotten Son. He is the substance of your unseen majesty. In Him, like a rare jewel, you show us all the gleaming facets of your wisdom—throwing sparks of your Light higher than the heavens, and into the deepest of all depths.

Lord Jesus, so mighty is your purity!

Jesus . . . delicate touch . . . Word . . . Son of God! You are the One who walks silently in the innermost sanctuary of our soul. So carefully you weave yourself into the fibers of our being. You take us into yourself, without degrading, without destroying. We lose ourselves and lose nothing at all, for your ways are beyond all telling.

Touch me, then, with your cleansing, renewing fire, O Word! Make my spirit pure and simple and light, as you are. Give my soul wings. Let me rise with the dawning of each day, closer to my heavenly land, nearer to the feast you are preparing.

On your Spirit's sweetest winds, Lord, you have set my spirit free.

LIVING FLAME OF LOVE: STANZA 2

DAVID HAZARD developed the REKINDLING THE INNER FIRE devotional series to encourage others to keep the "heart" of their faith alive and afire with love for God. He also feels a special need to help Christians of today to "meet" men and women of the past whose experience of God belongs to the whole Church, for all the ages.

Hazard is an award-winning writer, the author of books for both adults and children, with international bestsellers among his many titles. He lives in northern Virginia with his wife, MaryLynne, and three children: Aaron, Joel, and Sarah Beth.